PERSONAL FINANCE

fastread
PERSONAL FINANCE

Learn how to manage, save, and invest your money!

Adams Media Corporation

Holbrook, Massachusetts

product manager: Gary Krebs
series editor: Michelle Roy Kelly
production director: Susan Beale
production coordinator: Debbie Sidman
series designer: Daria Perreault
layout and graphics: Arlene Apone, Paul Beatrice,
Colleen Cunningham, Frank Rivera

Published by
Adams Media Corporation
260 Center Street, Holbrook, MA 02343, U.S.A.
www.adamsmedia.com

ISBN: 1-58062-510-X

Printed in Canada.

J I H G F E D C B A

Fastread personal finance: understand managing, saving, and investing money!
p. cm.
ISBN: 1-58062-510-X
1. Finance, Personal. 2. Investments. I. Title: Personal finance. II. Adams Media
Corporation.
HG179 .F368 2001
332.024--dc21

2001022809

This publication is designed to provide accurate and authoritative information with
regard to the subject matter covered. It is sold with the understanding that the publisher
is not engaged in rendering legal, accounting, or other professional advice. If legal
advice or other expert assistance is required, the services of a competent professional
person should be sought.

—From a *Declaration of Principles* jointly adopted
by a Committee of the American Bar Association
and a Committee of Publishers and Associations

Many of the designations used by manufacturers and sellers to distinguish their
products are claimed as trademarks. Where those designations appear in this book and
Adams Media was aware of a trademark claim, the designations have been printed in
initial capital letters.

This book is available at quantity discounts for bulk purchases.
For information, call 1-800-872-5627.

Visit our exciting home page at www.fastread.com

contents

introduction ix

chapter one 1

Personal Budgets

Getting Started 1

Budget Categories 2

Calculating a Budget 6

Sample Family Budget 7

Budgeting for Milestones 8

Shopping 8

Personal Finances and Your PC 10

chapter two 13

Credit Cards

How Credit Cards Work 14

Choosing a Credit Card 15

Lost or Stolen Credit Cards 19
Your Credit Rating 19

chapter three 25
Debt
Staying Out of Debt 26
Bailing Out 27
Personal Bankruptcy 31
Two Forms of Bankruptcy 31

chapter four 35
Basic Banking
Interest 37
Types of Accounts 37
Certificates of Deposit (CDs) 39
U.S. Treasury Bills 40
How to Choose a Bank 41
Balancing Your Checkbook 43
Online Banking 44

chapter five 47
Stocks
Stock Basics 48
Stocks and You 51
Choosing Stocks 52
Stock Market Indicators 53
Buying Stocks 54
Care to Drip or Dip? 55
Other Considerations When Buying Stocks 56
Choosing a Broker or Brokerage House 57
Online Trading 59
Systems and Strategies 61

chapter six 65
Mutual Funds
Risk Versus Reward and Risk Versus Tolerance 66
Stock Funds 68
Bond Funds 69
Money Market Mutual Funds 70
Balanced Funds 70
Load Versus No-Load Funds 71
Read the Prospectus 72
So Many to Choose From 73
Keeping Track 74
Fund Managers 75

chapter seven 77
Bonds
Types of Bonds 79
Bond Ratings 82

chapter eight 83
Retirement and Estate Planning
Social Security 83
Medicare 85
Your Retirement Plan 85
Handling Money During Retirement 91
Five Retirement Options to Consider 92
Estate Planning 93
The Will 94
Probate 94
Trusts 95
Gifting 97

chapter nine 99
Taxes
Filling Out the Forms 100
Reducing and Avoiding Taxes 102
Quarterly Versus Yearly Payments 103
Extensions 104
State and Local Taxes 105
Working with the IRS 105

chapter ten 107
Additional Information
Financial Web Sites 107
Retirement Planning Information 108
American Association of Individual Investors 109
National Association of Personal Finance Advisors . . 110
Tax Information 110

index 113

introduction

Money is an integral part of our lives and to be in control of its effects on your present and future is a significant step towards happiness. Although a great amount of wealth would be nice, a firm handle on your financial affairs can be almost as satisfying. Security. Comfort. Peace of mind. All these things can be achieved through effective money management. This book is designed to help you manage, maintain, and increase the money you have.

Money management is more than just creating a budget, though that is an important task. It encompasses not only day to day living, but planning for long-term financial security as well. It takes continuous work and restructuring. Life changes frequently and your money management system should change right along with it. Though it may seem as though the process is detailed and overwhelming, the concept is relatively simple: Maintain control of your money, or your money will control you.

There are several ways in which you can master your financial affairs. The choice is yours. Regardless of the path you choose, it is important to establish financial goals and set up strategies to meet these goals. As your life changes, you may have to re-evaluate and even alter your plans, but it's worth your while to set up a realistic plan incorporating both control over daily financial affairs and an approach for long-term financial gain. What you must keep in mind is that this plan is derived from personal choices. No two people will have the exact same desires and needs; therefore, using a ready-made system will likely create more problems than it solves. On the other hand, starting from scratch will create unnecessary stress and frustration. Ideally, you can use a sample plan and tailor it to suit your needs.

Though each system has its own disposition, there are a few keys to effective money management that are universal:

1. Keep good records in a simple filing system.
2. Know your current financial picture at any given time.
3. Be aware of your spending habits.
4. Know your financial priorities and goals.

From budgeting to investing to retirement and estate planning, this book is a practical guide anyone can refer to while managing personal finances. It will touch upon all areas that involve you and your hard-earned money. You need only to plan ahead, consider your future goals, and determine how you can best achieve them.

chapter one

Personal Budgets

Getting Started

Creating a personal budget is the first and most important way to get a firm handle on your financial affairs. A budget is an ongoing financial statement that will help you stay in control of your money and keep you on track. Because it allows you to compare your income with expenditures, you can easily make adjustments to create a system of priorities. Once these are in place, you will be able to gauge how much money is available for investments and any other financial goals you have set.

The first step is to take a close look at your overall financial picture. In the never-ending battle between assets and liabilities, which is winning?

Assets include all of your current bank accounts, mutual funds, money market accounts, securities, bonds, and treasury bills. Also included are life insurance policies, retirement accounts, and personal property. On the other side of the ledger are the liabilities, which include all outstanding debts, monthly bills, mortgage payments, long-term loans, and unpaid taxes. Your net worth is the difference between the liabilities and the assets.

Next, you should establish a system of record keeping so that you can assess your net worth and create a budget that gives you a solid indicator of where you stand financially at any given time. Whether you are using a notebook or a computer program, it is important for tax purposes, as well as for backup purposes, that you keep copies of all your receipts, canceled checks, pay stubs, and all other paperwork accompanying your income and expenses. Should you lose a page of your budget, have a computer glitch, or a tax audit, good record keeping and backup files are vital.

A good budget will show both monthly and yearly allowances. If your annual budget is broken down into months, you'll have an ongoing statement of how you are doing financially at any given point in time. This allows you to compare how much you are earning with how much you are spending in a particular area and make adjustments before the year ends. At the end of the year, you will be able to adjust for the following year by placing a plus or minus sign next to the annual totals in comparison to your budgeted amounts.

A well-structured budget will be easy to follow, suit your lifestyle, leave room for expansion, and help you to meet your financial goals.

Budget Categories

Income

Income includes your net paycheck (your take-home pay after withholding taxes and social security). If, however, your primary source of income is derived from freelancing or any other means of self-employment, list your total income, then subtract estimated self-employment taxes in your expense column.

Other sources of income include bonuses, tips, royalties, stock dividends, interest, trust funds, disability benefits, veterans benefits, inheritance, alimony, child support, and even gifts and gambling winnings. Any definite income source should be included. Investments will fall on both sides of your budget. Unfortunately, you cannot know in advance (other than dividends) which investments will land on the income side. Therefore, you should list investments as an expense, since it is not money you can utilize at the present time.

Expenses

Your budget should have a column for everything you will routinely spend money on, extra columns for specific areas you might add, and a miscellaneous category for unforeseen expenses.

There are two categories of expenses: fixed and variable expenses. First, list your fixed expenses. These are the ones that will not change from month to month. They can also be once-a-year payments that are predetermined.

Fixed expenses

- Rent/Mortgage payment
- Loans—This includes automobile loans, student loans, and any other loans that are a fixed amount. If you have several loans, you may want to break down this category even further.
- Insurance—This includes renters' insurance, automobile insurance, and any other insurance such as medical that is not already deducted from your gross pay.

Next, list your variable expenses. These will fluctuate from month to month based on usage.

Variable expenses

- Weekly living—This includes food from the grocery store, dining out, snacks, and sundry goods including toiletries and the multitude of items that fill your medicine cabinet and linen closet.
- Utilities—Gas, telephone, electric, heating, water, and cable bills that vary monthly fall into this category. Some of these bills may have a basic monthly rate, but most will differ depending on amount of use.
- Automobile—This includes gas, repair, and maintenance. Do not add your car or insurance payment here, since you have already included that in the fixed expenses category.
- Credit Cards— If you have several credit cards, you may decide to break down this category into individual cards in order to itemize your debts.
- Travel/Vacation— Include all of the tolls you pay getting to and from work and wherever else you routinely travel. Any travel-related expenses that your employer does not cover should be included here. As for vacations, don't be surprised when hotels, airfare, food, and entertainment costs total up to a bit more than you anticipated. Determine your financial picture, and plan your vacation accordingly.
- Home-related—Aside from the fixed cost of rent or a mortgage, you need to consider the cost of furniture and home improvements. Some of this will be "discretionary" spending, but a lot of the upkeep of a house is ongoing and necessary, such as preparation for winter in certain areas or repainting. Even though the money you spend now on improving your home may raise its value in the long run, it is currently an expense.
- Clothing (including shoes and accessories)—Your clothing expenditure will depend largely on where you work, your lifestyle, and the impression you need to

make. Don't forget to include laundry and dry-cleaning expenses.

- Entertainment and recreation—CD players, VCRs, and trips to the movies, the theater, the ballet, and the ballpark all count as entertainment. You may also include books, magazines, or hobby expenses in this category.
- Gifts and charitable contributions—List whatever you give. This category adds up, especially around the holidays. Include donations as well as personal gifts to family and friends and note if they are tax-deductible.
- Savings—Although the money is still yours, money set aside for savings is considered an expense, if only in that you can't spend it, at least for the time being. However, if a portion of your paycheck is in a direct deposit savings account, then you need not list it at all, assuming you are listing your income after such money has been taken out.
- Miscellaneous—This category is for incidental expenses that don't quite fit anywhere else. There will inevitably be a few unexpected expenses that will fall into this category. For instance, this column might include medications, medical related equipment (including glasses), and doctor's fees that aren't covered in your insurance plan.

If you have difficulty reaching an estimated amount for a category, then chart all your expenses for two weeks prior to setting up that category in the budget. This should give you a good idea of how much you are spending. These categories are by no means set in stone. Rather, this is simply a sample of one way in which you might divide the budget. Budgets should be tailored to the individual. Whereas a budget for a mother of three might include child care, piano lessons, and education, a single man might not have any use for those categories.

Use whatever divisions and combinations you are comfortable with when creating a budget. However, do make sure that once you determine which category to use you are consistent. If your car payment is in two separate categories, that one mistake will throw the entire budget off track.

Calculating a Budget

Initially calculated from monthly amounts, your budget should show how much money is needed annually in each category. Then, on a monthly basis, you should keep running totals and divide by the number of months to see how you are doing.

For example, if you estimate, that you will spend $90 monthly on transportation, your total for that year would be $1,080. Some of us like to play it safe and budget to a higher number, usually increased by about 10 percent. Thus, you might list $1,200 as your annual transportation budget. Suppose that at the end of March your three-month total is $480. You would divide the total by three months and find that your monthly total is actually $160. That would put you at $1,920, or $720 over your annual budget. Your options would be to either find a less expensive mode of transportation or find another budget area that is running under and readjust your amounts.

Although the first option may not be practical, the second should work. By keeping track and looking for ways to readjust your budget, you can solve the problem. Keep in mind that you shouldn't jump to conclusions based on one month. Don't be fooled by seasonal changes or other factors that can cause a category to shift. For example, if your electric bills are lower in January and February, think twice before lowering the budgeted amount for electricity. Otherwise, you may be surprised when the summer comes and the air conditioner raises your electric bill. In short, keep a solid gauge on what is going on monthly.

Sample Family Budget

INCOME:	ANNUAL	MONTHLY
His annual income (net pay)	$37,500	$3,125
Her annual income (net pay)	$37,500	$3,125
Stocks/savings accounts	$3,000	$250
Investment, capital gains	$3,000	$250
Subtotal	**$81,000**	**$6,750**

EXPENSES	ANNUAL	MONTHLY
Rent/Mortgage	$18,000	$1,500
Loans	$6,000	$500
Insurance Premiums	$3,000	$250
Weekly living	$15,000	$250
Utilities	$4,500	$375
Automobile	$5,100	$425
Credit cards	$2,400	$200
Travel/Vacation	$2,400	$200
Home related	$3,600	$300
Clothing	$6,000	$500
Entertainment	$6,000	$500
Gifts and Charity	$1,500	$125
Savings	$3,000	$250
Miscellaneous	$1,500	$125
Total	**$78,000**	**$6,500**
Available cash	$3,000	$250

There are several ways you can set up your budget. This sample budget includes the income of both partners in a two-income family, in addition to the money earned from stocks, savings accounts, and one other investment. At the end of the year, if they stay on their budget, they will have $3,000 left over to do with as they please.

Budgeting for Milestones

Planning for weddings, vacations, and other major events means you will need to adjust your budget for a specific period of time. Make a new column for this event in your annual budget. If you factor in an estimated amount at the start of the year, you can better determine what you can afford.

A good idea in preparing for any potential major expense is to set up a savings plan with enough advance time to allow your money to work for you. Also allow for inflation, as costs will be higher for a wedding in five years than they are now.

Shopping

Beyond the major purchases, such as a home and a car, there are numerous other items on which you can spend your hard-earned cash. Washers, dryers, stereos, televisions, furniture, recreational and fitness equipment, computers, and numerous other goods make up our vast consumer spending index. This area is where you can run into trouble. The trick is to be selective and focus on the things you really feel are important to your lifestyle. We all need most of the above mentioned items; the question is, how many and at what price? This is where your budget should guide you, not restrict you. The careful, smart shopper can purchase a significant amount of items without spending a fortune.

Buying guides such as *Consumer Reports* will tell you what the best rated products are, but then it's up to you to look around for the best prices. Browsing the Internet, reading newspapers, and on occasion, simply waiting until the newest fad is no longer the hottest selling item are ways of saving money when you shop. When a new product hits the market, it is always priced higher.

The idea is not to be "cheap" but to be savvy and to spend top dollar only on selected items or where time is of the essence.

Impulse buying is another route to debt and trouble. For major purchases, it is sometimes a good idea to tell yourself to wait three days and then, if you still feel you need the item, buy it. You'd be surprised how many "must have" impulse items are less appealing a few days later.

Always buy through reputable retailers. Too often, lesser known mail order companies don't have the item you want and persuade you to select something else. They also have different pricing in different parts of the country. Often these companies go out of business, sometimes holding onto your money. Those that do send you merchandise are not always sending the highest quality goods.

Here are some other shopping tips:

- You get what you pay for. Brand names may be more costly, but (depending on the item) you usually get higher quality merchandise.
- It's usually not in your best interests to buy extended warranties offered by the merchandiser. Warranties from the manufacturer usually cover the first year or two

already. And according to retailers surveyed, less than 20 percent of the warranties sold are ever put to use.

- While it's important to shop at reputable companies, it's also important to deal with merchandisers that specialize in the type of product you are buying. Shop in the right stores.
- It's also a good idea to get everything in writing, save receipts, and double check the return and exchange policy on whatever you purchase.

Personal Finances and Your PC

You can use your PC to manage your personal finances. From budgets, record keeping, and banking to investing and planning your financial future, your computer can be your own financial resource center. Most programs will help you by doing basic calculations quickly and allowing you to compare your current data with that of previous months or years—providing you've entered them.

The two leading programs in the area of personal finance are Quicken from Intuit and Money from Microsoft. While each presents their new annual editions, you need to assess before upgrading which features, if any, you may need. Quite often, new editions will include features that are impressive yet unnecessary. Look for a program that doesn't require that you change your approach to finance management.

There are various other programs devoted to personal budgets and finance, such as MECA Software's Managing Your Money. Long-time spreadsheet programs such as Excel or even Lotus can be used as well, should you already have them on your computer. Although not as comprehensive as some of the budgeting programs, they provide spreadsheets and do basic calculations.

How much you involve your computer in your financial matters is ultimately a question of your own comfort level. Computers can "run the whole show," provided you are at the controls. Many people, however, find that they are still most comfortable with a combination in which they utilize their computer for record keeping, budgeting, and even checkbook balancing, but still do their own banking and bill paying. The decision is entirely a matter with personal preference.

chapter two

Credit Cards

Our society has become somewhat reliant upon credit cards. Several hotels will not accept a reservation without one. It is difficult, if not impossible, in some places to rent a car without a credit card. From department stores to gas stations to the local food emporium, every retail outlet, catalog, home shopping network, and Internet site will offer you the chance to pay using your credit card. They make shopping from home via computer or television very easy. One little piece of plastic can give you tremendously increased purchasing power.

Credit cards can benefit you in many ways. They are a convenient way to avoid carrying around a lot of cash. You can also get a number of freebies including frequent flier mileage, discounts for hotels and rental cars, gift certificates, and other benefits. But in order to get the most enjoyment out of their use, you must handle them wisely and responsibly.

Credit cards can also mean trouble. Too many individuals end up spending money they don't have. Spend now, pay later is the basic premise of credit cards. The individual who, by his or her nature, seeks instant gratification is more likely to run into credit card debt than the person who plans ahead.

If you are on the brink of falling behind on your credit card payments, you can easily turn it around by becoming stricter with yourself. You need to start making rules to guide you.

You could, for example, employ a rule that you use credit cards only for major expenses and in emergencies. Keep track each month of how much is in your checking account (or can be moved immediately into the account) to cover each large purchase ($300 or more). Then make a note of all credit card transactions and keep an eye on the checking account balance, since it will be from there that you pay the credit card bill.

If you are one of the many suffering under the weight of credit card debt, there are steps you can take to get back on your feet. There will be more information on credit card debt in the next chapter.

How Credit Cards Work

It's in your best interest to understand how the credit card industry works. The more you know, the better you'll understand why it's important to be responsible with these cards.

Basically, the issuer, be it a bank, store, or other institution, extends you a loan to buy goods or services. They may set a limit, such as $2,000 to start with, meaning that that's the maximum you can borrow from them at any given time. You receive a monthly bill, and if you pay it in full and on time, you do not incur other charges. However, if you don't pay in full, the interest rate can be as high as 20 or 22 percent.

Although many credit card companies offer special services, usually to "preferred customers" with high-credit limits, it is worth your while (if you do not feel confident that you will pay in full every month) to seek out low-interest-rate cards, even if they do not offer frequent flier mileage and other such amenities. Some credit card companies charge annual fees. They may offer various services and their interest rates may be lower, but you still pay a fee for the convenience of spending without using cash.

Choosing a Credit Card

Treat your options for a credit card just as you would any major purchase. Take your time and compare. Credit card requirements, set by the issuer, vary significantly. Though special discounts offered may appeal to you, it's best to first take a look at the payment features. This information is normally found in the fine print under Terms and Conditions. Knowing these conditions is well worth the eye strain.

- The interest rate is probably one of the first things to catch your eye, especially with several cards advertising too-good-to-be-true low rates. However, this interest rate is usually offered only during a specified introductory period. Depending on how long you plan to utilize the card, this offer could be ideal for you. For most of us though, the life of the card extends well beyond the introductory period. It's best to read the fine print to find out the stipulations regarding these low interest rates. Sometimes they apply only to balances transferred from other cards. Sometimes they will even last only a month. Find out what the interest rate is normally. Also, keep in mind that fixed rates can also be increased.
- It also helps to know how the interest is being calculated. Interest is usually figured using the average daily balance,

adjusted balance, or previous balance. However, keep an eye out for plans proposing two-cycle balances. This method charges interest on purchases made during the previous billing cycle. In other words, you are being charged interest on interest already accrued.

- Nearly every credit card charges a fee for one reason or another. Pay special attention to all these seemingly harmless fees. They can add up quickly. The most common are late payment, overlimit, annual, and transaction fees. Others include inactivity fees imposed when you have had no transactions within a certain amount of time, fees charged with the acceptance of a credit limit increase, and even penalties imposed when you pay off your balance.
- The grace period is the amount of time you have to pay off the balance before a finance charge is imposed. For those expecting to pay your account in full each month, this information is especially important.

Read the fine print carefully, do not accept the card without first understanding the Terms and Conditions. There are numerous cards out there offering a variety of services and plans. Though the work may be tedious, it pays off in the long run to find a card that best suits your needs.

The most popular credit cards offered today are Visa and MasterCard. Companies, banks, and corporations sponsor these cards. Both of these cards extend to you a line of credit. You can pay them back at your own pace, but you will incur interest on the amount owed and, possibly, additional charges.

The American Express card works like a charge card, but unlike a line of credit, American Express essentially pays the bill for you. Therefore, the cardholder is not allowed to pay in increments. The balance must be paid in full for whatever was charged at the end of the 30-day cycle. They make money on the fees they charge to merchants and the yearly fees they charge to cardholders. However, American Express also offers the Optima card, which allows you to make monthly payments in the same manner as Visa and MasterCard.

Be sure to look at what privileges cards offer, such as frequent flier mileage, savings on long-distance calls, store discounts, and so on. Be careful that "extras" don't have fees or other requirements attached. Some companies offer to help you do practically anything, anyplace in the world. They fail, however, to remind you that you may have to sign up for this special service in advance or charge up to a certain amount on the card. Many of these rewards are only offered on certain cards such as gold cards or platinum cards.

It's to your advantage to stick to a few credit cards that you know you will actually use and can pay in full at the end of the month. Don't be taken in by everyone who wants to send you a free credit card—this only leads to too many cards and can be your credit downfall (not to mention the paperwork of sending out payments and keeping track of them all). If you apply for a card every time you receive an application in the mail, it will be marked down on your credit rating or credit report. Applying for many cards can make a lender nervous because they see that you could run up a large amount of debt. They will be less likely to extend you credit if they think you already owe several others.

The benefits and offers of competing cards is mind boggling. Gold/platinum/titanium cards offer more benefits (accrue frequent flier mileage faster, rental insurance, purchase protection) than normal cards but also have higher annual membership fees. Cash back cards (Discover, US West MasterCard) offer money back based on the level of purchases. Hotel cards (Caesar's Gold MasterCard, Marriott First Card) offer points towards discounts on dining, entertainment, merchandise, and hotel stays.

The list goes on and on. There are cards offering discounts for everything you could possibly want. Shop around. If you are a frequent flier, look for frequent flier mileage; if you are going on vacation, seek out hotel or car rental deals. You can pick and choose cards that have good interest rates, extend you a substantial credit limit, and have perks or extras that are tailored for your lifestyle.

Secured credit cards (cards that require a deposit in advance) are good for building up a credit rating (showing you can pay on time). If you want to acquire other credit cards, apply for a loan, or get a mortgage, a secured credit card is a good starting point. Get secured cards only through reputable financial institutions directly. Don't hand over your deposit to a unknown company.

Keep in mind that after you have carefully compared and selected a card, you still need to monitor its terms. Don't throw away those extra papers buried within the advertisements that accompany your statement each month. Chances are, the credit card company is sending you notifications of changes of their terms. The original agreement can be changed. By law, the issuer is required to send only 15 days notice. By keeping up with the change in terms, you will be able to save money otherwise needlessly spent.

Debit cards, the opposite of a credit card, deduct the amount of your purchase directly from your bank account. If you do not have the money in the account, the charge will not go through, thus eliminating the possibility for you to go over your limit and mount up interest charges. Visa, MasterCard, and other companies offer debit cards, but they are not nearly as widely hyped, simply because the companies can make more money off you by watching you run your credit card bills sky high.

ATM bank cards can also be used as debit cards. These have become increasingly more popular in recent years. It's worth inquiring when opening a bank account whether the bank can issue you a debit card or if you can use your ATM card as such. Be aware that some banks charge a fee for using an ATM card as a charge. Find out your bank's terms.

Lost or Stolen Credit Cards

Keep the toll-free number of the issuer of your card handy in the event your card is lost or stolen. Copy it down and keep it with your phone numbers at home. If the card is lost or stolen, report it immediately so that the issuer can cancel the card. You will not be billed for subsequent charges to your card. If the card has already been used, you may be liable for a small amount.

You should always review your credit card bill carefully, since it's important to note any charges that obviously do not belong to you. People have discovered that they lost their credit card(s) by noting such erroneous charges on their bills. Also, through phone sales as well as other means—such as copying the imprint of your card (many places have more updated systems to avoid this)—good scam artists can get your credit card number and charge items to your account. Most major credit card companies have no problem voiding such payments, if you've established a good credit rating. If erroneous charges show up with any frequency, cancel the card and get a new one. An alert credit card company will call you or even request identification at the point of purchase if the card is used for a series of transactions in a short period of time.

Your Credit Rating

Your credit rating follows you around throughout your life. It can help you make a major purchase if your credit is good and work against you if the rating is not good.

To qualify for credit and loans, you'll need to prove yourself worthy in the eyes of the lenders. Biased as it may seem, especially in this day and age of companies merging and new opportunities allowing (sometimes forcing) people to make several job changes, lenders like to see that you have stayed at one job for a period of time. They like to see that your bills are paid on time. They also want to know all about your assets, earnings, and investments. They try to cover all bases when determining whether you are a good bet when it comes to borrowing money or extending a line of credit. Many credit card companies make it fairly easy to qualify for their card because they want as many cardholders as possible. In many cases, they are satisfied knowing you can come close to meeting your monthly balance.

Your credit report is tracked by a credit bureau. The credit bureau doesn't write the credit reports; it simply takes in and assimilates the information given by the companies with which you do business. It then sells your personal information to potential credit grantors. Anyone making transactions has some credit bureau keeping tabs on their payment history and habits. Through stores, banks, financial institutions, and other means, the credit bureau builds up a report on you that will be checked when you apply for a credit card, apartment, or mortgage.

If you want to build a good credit rating, start with a store credit card; they are usually easy to acquire. Another option is to start with a secured card, as mentioned earlier. Once you start with a low limit and pay off your bills on time, you will begin to build a good credit report, get higher credit limits, and qualify for more cards.

There are three major companies handling credit ratings in the United States: Trans Union, Experian, and Equifax. You have a right, by law, to see your credit report.

You may very well be listed with two or all three of the credit bureaus, since different businesses work with the three companies.

It's a good idea to check all three credit ratings, especially if you are about to buy a home or make some other significant purchase involving a loan or mortgage.

Don't be surprised if they differ. Also, don't be surprised if there's an error. Due to the incredibly large number of people listed (nearly two hundred million in the United States), errors are made. Errors are more commonly made by a merchant incorrectly reporting your purchases or failing to report that you've paid off a delinquent bill. You must prove that an error is just that. Common mistakes include putting someone else's information on your form and neglecting to list follow-up information on a loan that you have paid. Getting errors corrected is a long and tedious process. Get something in writing and make sure to notify all the credit bureaus. Be polite but persistent, as it's important to have credit rating errors corrected while maintaining your good name.

Because errors are rather common and your credit rating has a significant impact on your life, it is advised that you get a copy of your credit report once a year. Look it over carefully and don't postpone correcting an error.

These are the "big three" credit bureaus:

Equifax
Credit Information Services
P.O. Box 105496
Atlanta, GA 30348-5496
800/997-2493
www.equifax.com

Experian
National Consumer Assistance Center
P.O. Box 2104
Allen, TX 75013
888/EXPERIAN
www.experian.com

Trans Union LLC
Consumer Disclosure Center
P.O. Box 1000
Chester, PA 19022
800/888-4213
www.transunion.com

If an error has not been corrected or you cannot get satisfactory results from a credit bureau, call either the office of the attorney general in your state or the Federal Trade Commission in Washington, DC.

Essentially, a good credit rating, like a good report card, is a plus. Showing that you are responsible when it concerns money matters is the most significant step. For the most part, however, the idea that you can stay within your means is the key. There are minor delinquencies and major delinquencies when paying off credit. Someone who is late paying three bills and then recovers and is consistent about paying their bills from that point forward will show a minor delinquency. This can happen because of a life crisis and is not usually frowned upon. However, if a debt is turned over to a collection agency or the company has listed it as bad debt or a loss, you fall into the major delinquency category, also known as a major derogatory. Either way you are in big trouble creditwise.

Delinquencies stay on your report for seven years after they have been paid off. Outstanding debts remain on your report until they are paid off.

To keep yourself on track, look at what creditors look for:

1. Missed payments. Creditors examine how often you miss a payment, how long ago you missed it, and whether you have outstanding payments. They also look to see whether you have a consistent level of debt

and the amount of debt versus your credit limit. For instance, if you owe $1,000 but your credit limit is $10,000, that's a low percentage of the amount of debt that you could have accrued. However, if you owe $9,000, or 90 percent, they will be more leery about offering you more credit.

2. Time of credit. If you've been a credit card holder for twenty years and have paid your bill late only five times, it's not significant.

3. How much debt you could have. The other aspect that comes into play in your credit report is how much debt you have and how much you could have tomorrow. If you keep opening accounts, there is a greater risk you could be in debt tomorrow. Your spending habits then become more consequential.

The best way to avoid a wealth of debt and a bad credit report is not to get into trouble in the first place. Fight the urge. Don't overspend on your cards!

chapter three

Debt

Debt today is due in large part to consumerism and the amount of goods and services easily available. Products and services are all around us, and credit cards make them more easily accessible than ever before. However, people need to take some responsibility for their spending habits. It's important to determine what you can and cannot afford, either at present or at the end of the month, when your credit card bill shows up in your mailbox. Essentially every time you use your credit card, you are taking out a loan. If you were to ask someone to lend you $20 for gas every time you needed to fill the tank, you would know that you owe this person money and that the amount is adding up. However, the plastic card makes it easy to forget because the lender is an anonymous source.

Staying Out of Debt

For those who are worried about heading into debt, you can evaluate your current situation and determine ways to avoid it. Here are some suggestions:

- Keep a close watch on your monthly or weekly spending.
- Avoid using credit cards for small items.
- Make sure you have money set aside to cover your credit card payments and pay in full at the end of each month.
- The first month you fall behind on your payments, change your spending habits.
- Take out loans only for major purchases, such as car or home buying, and make the monthly payment with interest your top priority when you get paid.
- Borrow only for emergencies.
- Develop a plan of putting aside money so that you always have some reserve.
- Shop wisely and seek out good deals; avoid impulse buying and think about what you really want and need.
- If you're not good at disciplining yourself and handling money wisely, have it deposited directly into your account.
- If you do go into debt, do not assume that if you ignore it, it will go away.

Amazingly enough, the last item is one of the most frequent causes of personal bankruptcy and major debt-related headaches. It is very common for people to avoid their debt, change the subject, throw the pile of bills into the drawer, or even tear them up. But, this kind of action will not make the problem disappear. Bills need to be paid, and there's no way around it. In addition, interest fees continue to accumulate. If you see debt staring you in the face, stare back and fight; if you try to ignore it, you'll end up digging yourself into deeper trouble.

Bailing Out

If you find that you are already in debt, there are ways to start bailing yourself out. As mentioned earlier, credit cards make it easy to slip into substantial debt. Though you may think you have become a slave to the credit card companies, you can regain control.

Before you take that first step towards financial freedom, you must assess the damage. Know exactly how much debt you are carrying with each creditor. Then add them all together for a grand total (this can help to motivate you into action).

The best strategy for eliminating credit card debt will vary depending on how much you owe and your current financial situation. However, the first step remains the same—stop spending. You won't be able to decrease the amount owed if you keep adding to it.

Carry some cash at all times. When you consider it, the purchases you make normally cost less when paying with cash. Even losing $100 by misplacing your wallet or purse is a small "investment" compared with throwing thousands of dollars into interest charges and late payment fees. Also, most people will have the tendency to spend less when they actually see the money leaving their hands.

Next, review your options. You can transfer all your credit card balances onto one low-interest card. If you choose to do this, be sure to read the fine print. That low interest rate may sky rocket within a few months making the finance charge even greater than what you were paying before. Also keep in mind that credit card companies frequently change the terms of agreement with very little notice.

Another option is to prioritize your credit card payments. Start with paying off the highest interest rate card first. You should try to pay as much over the minimum as possible with this card and maintain the minimum on all other cards. Because the high interest eats up the amount actually going towards the bill, the sooner you get this one paid off, the more money you will save in the long run.

After paying off the first card (don't forget to close the account with the company, or you might incur charges), move to the second highest interest card. Add the money you had assigned to the first card to the minimum of the second card, and so on. You will see that once you get the ball rolling, the debts will drop rather quickly.

If you find that you simply can't make your payments, contact the creditors. If you are honest and explain your financial situation, more than likely they will work with you to create a plan that is manageable. However, be sure to contact them before your account is turned over to a debt collector. Also, don't contact one and not the others. Try to pay each creditor something, regardless of how small the amount. This shows good faith and they will be more willing to work with you if they see that you are sincerely trying to pay off the debt. The bottom line is that they want their money.

You also have the option of consolidating your credit cards and loans into one loan. Advantages of this plan are that you will be paying only one creditor and will be able to better track how much you have left to pay off. Also, the monthly payments are normally lower than what you are currently paying. However, there are also disadvantages to this type of plan. Along with the lowered monthly payments comes an extended payment period accompanied by high interest rates. Debt consolidation loans are often secured by either collateral such as your house, or by a co-signer. Either way, you have a lot to lose if you were to default.

Take your time and carefully review the short-term and long-term pros and cons of a debt consolidation loan as a means to better your financial situation.

Alternative Actions

Borrowing from friends and family works for a short time. Initially, good friends may be happy to help you if they can afford to. Over time, however, this resource, and possibly your friendship, will dissolve. Pretty soon people won't be so quick to return your phone calls. Here are some important considerations when borrowing from family and friends:

1. Look to borrow from people who are financially sound. Thus, you can avoid the awkward situation in which someone says, "I'd love to lend you the money, but I don't have it myself."
2. Borrow money only for specific needs.
3. Write up an agreement, no matter how basic, detailing how much you're borrowing and when you anticipate paying it back.
4. From time to time, remind the lender that you are aware of the loan.
5. Pay off the loan as soon as you can.

You can also borrow against your assets, the biggest of which is your home, if you have home equity. Home equity is the difference between the value of the house and the remaining loan balance, and can be the basis for a low interest loan. You may also own a cash value life insurance policy that you can borrow against.

Another option is to sell off or cash in investments, starting with those that do not hit you with penalties. If the debt is just starting to accumulate, you might be able to nip it in the bud by selling off a few assets. Essentially, you can start slimming down assets much in the way the courts would do if you filed for bankruptcy, but your credit rating would not disappear and you'd have control over which assets you wanted to try to maintain.

You can, if possible, look for other ways to earn extra income that will be solely used to pay off the debt. From part-time tutoring to actual moonlighting, there are probably ways in which you can earn a few extra dollars to get out of debt, if you move while it's still a reasonable amount.

Professional Credit Help

If you feel that getting out of debt is too overwhelming and that you cannot do it alone, there are organizations you can contact to help you. Make sure that the person you work with is a proven professional. Amateurs can get you in even more credit trouble, and scam artists can simply rip you off, since you are vulnerable. Credit fixers have a number of offbeat approaches to correcting your low credit rating, such as creating a new line of credit for you under a "new" identity. This is illegal, as are most of their "bright ideas." Avoid credit fixers!

Before you do business with any agency that promises to help you get out of debt, check them out with the Better Business Bureau or a local consumer protection agency. See what other consumers have had to say about their services. Also it's good to get written verification of the services offered and what the costs are from the company. Be cautious, but don't be discouraged.

There are legitimate counselors and groups that work with people who are having a problem with spending and are in debt. The National Foundation for Consumer Credit (NFCC) (800/388-2227 or *www.nfcc.org*) is a good place to turn for credit education and counseling. With nearly fifteen hundred offices in the United States and Canada, the NFCC offers thousands of educational programs each year on budgeting and credit management to more than a million families.

A counselor will look over your credit card invoices, see where your balances are, and put you on a program. A counselor can also call your lenders and ask them to waive the late charges or other additional fees and even reduce the interest rate. Often it is to the lenders' benefit to help you at this juncture, because if you end up filing for personal bankruptcy, the interest rates will be waived and they'll receive less than 100 percent on the dollar.

Personal Bankruptcy

The last resort, should you find yourself in tremendous debt, is to file for personal bankruptcy. Filing for bankruptcy is usually best advised when your debt has exceeded your annual income and is growing at a faster rate than your potential future income. It is also recommended when you are being sued by creditors. It is, however, a decision that must be well thought out and handled carefully by a good bankruptcy attorney, not someone advertising that they can solve all your problems. In fact, a good bankruptcy attorney will be the one who first looks to find other alternatives. One of the problems today is that too many people jump the gun and file at the recommendation of an overanxious attorney.

Two Forms of Bankruptcy

Should you decide that your only alternative is to file for bank-ruptcy, there are two options: You can file under a Chapter 7 or 13. As soon as you file, an automatic stay will be enforced. This means that there is a stop placed on any repossessions, garnish-ments, foreclosures, and utility shut-offs. This also forbids debt collectors from harassing you. No action can be taken against you until the courts have reached a decision.

Filing under a Chapter 7 involves liquidating your assets; you turn over the bulk of your assets (those that are not exempt by state or federal law) to the court, which sells them off to pay your creditors. All of your debt is discharged, and you do not use your future income to repay any remaining debt.

Each state has its own laws regarding exemptions or assets that cannot be sold off by the courts. Some states allow you to retain your house, but most include at least a portion of it as equity.

Keep in mind the liquidation is used to pay off your unsecured debts such as utility bills, credit cards, and medical bills. However, there are some unsecured debts that you retain responsibility for. These include child support, student loans, and some taxes. Though Chapter 7 will aid in the repayment of secured debts (those backed by collateral), most often these debts are still at the mercy of the creditors.

You should not try to hide assets by moving them into another area. It is not wise to try to fool the courts by hiding assets; fraud carries stiff penalties. Also, once you have entered into an agreement with a lender of any kind, from that agreement on, most of the money you've moved is fair game for your creditors. In other words, if you buy a home and then start sending $500 a month to a friend, the banks, if you ever declare bankruptcy, can go after the $500 monthly amount you sent to your friend, from the date the lending agreement was signed.

A Chapter 13 filing includes the taking of future disposable income and giving it to a trustee of the bankruptcy system who distributes the money to your creditors. The trustee then pays off your bills based on a payment schedule set up with your creditors. Depending on state laws, you often pay off less than the full amount on the dollar. For example, based on your income, you might be expected to pay only $30,000, over five years, of a $50,000 debt. The rest would then be dismissed. Creditors have to agree to the plan, and you can have up to five years (the average time is three years) to pay off the agreed-upon portion of the debt. You need to look at the earning capability of any disposable income, then you need to look at the asset base. This is feasible for someone who has fallen into debt but now has enough steady income to pay it back. As long as the payments are made, you get to keep all your property and are protected from foreclosure and repossession.

Personal bankruptcy is not pleasant. However, on a positive note, you are out of debt and can start again. All transactions are frozen in time when the papers are signed. Therefore, the creditors cannot come after you with a lawsuit. No more interest can be added, and nothing should be done by either party—the courts are in control at this point.

Bankruptcy will remain on your credit report for 10 years. This can make it very difficult to get loans or even a credit card in the future. Before filing, carefully consider the impact bankruptcy will have on, not only your present, but also your future financial affairs.

chapter four

Basic Banking

Though banks perform several services ranging from counseling to extending credit, the basic purpose of each is the same: to establish a safe place to keep your money. However, not all banks are protected equally. Check to make sure your bank has an official FDIC logo. The Federal Deposit Insurance Corporation (FDIC) insures each account for up to $100,000. While the vast majority of banks in the United States are FDIC affiliated, not all banks are covered.

If you're putting more than $100,000 in the bank, you need to put your funds in different ownership categories. Ownership is determined by what is shown on the "deposit of account records" of the insured depository institution. The "deposit of account records" are signature cards, account ledgers, certificates of deposits, passbooks, and certain computer records. Opening accounts at different banks is ideal. Using various accounts, such as a CD, a NOW account, and a savings account at the same bank, under your own name or ownership, won't do it.

Most types of deposits are covered by the FDIC including deposits in savings accounts, checking accounts, NOW accounts, Christmas accounts, CDs (certificates of deposit), cashiers checks, money orders, certified checks, and traveler's checks, issued in exchange for money.

Investments in mutual funds, stocks, bonds, T-bills, and/or money market mutual funds are not usually insured by the FDIC. Safety deposit boxes are also not protected by FDIC insurance.

The money you place in the hands of banks, primarily in the form of "cash investments," goes into savings accounts, checking accounts, money market accounts, NOW accounts, CDs, or miscellaneous other accounts. These cash accounts are significant because they set the foundation for moving toward riskier investments.

In cash accounts you are protected and cannot lose the principal. Interest rates vary, and determining which account will pay the highest rate of interest and over how much time is a tedious but worthwhile chore. Investments, on the other hand, are more popular than bank accounts because they pay higher interest rates, and it's not advisable to keep huge sums of money in the bank when you can find safe investment options.

One significant feature of a cash instrument, such as a NOW account, is that you can have your money "now," via check, ATM, or withdrawal. CDs, T-bills, and other investments tie your money up for a period of time. Therefore, for money you need on hand, look to your friendly neighborhood bank. This is where you establish your "cash flow," or the cash coming and going from your account on a daily basis.

Interest

The concept of having your money grow in any short- or long-term investment is based largely on the concept of interest: For the right to hold and use your money, you will be paid based on the rate of the type of investment you have selected. When putting money into an account, two important considerations are the interest rate and how often interest is compounded. The way in which money grows substantially over time is by compounding interest, that is, your interest keeps generating interest. The amount compounded (daily, monthly, or quarterly) will then grow and grow. Interest rates vary from bank to bank, but not by much.

Types of Accounts

Passbook/Statement Accounts

For many years, the most common bank account was the passbook savings account. It was the one account that offered interest (generally around 5 to 5.25 percent). You would take your passbook from your drawer or nightstand to the bank and have it stamped whenever you made a transaction.

Today such accounts still exist; however, statement accounts have become more popular. Now banks send you a monthly or quarterly statement. Such accounts generally pay 2 to 4 percent, and there are often minimum amounts required to maintain an account without having to pay extra bank charges.

Passbook or statement accounts are for those who don't meet the minimum for CDs or larger investments. They are for people who need liquidity, as well as for anyone who just finds them convenient and easy to understand.

Checking Accounts

A recent survey found that major banks now have an average of seven different types of checking accounts. For most of us, that's five or even six choices too many.

Negotiable order of withdrawal (NOW) accounts are the most commonly used checking accounts. Until recent years, checking accounts did not offer interest, but because of various competitive accounts and the vast number of banks, most checking accounts offer a low interest rate. Most NOW accounts allow for unlimited check writing but require you to keep a minimum balance of at least $500, $1,000, or $2,000. Some will allow you to have a minimum balance between several "linking" accounts; thus, if you have x amount of money between three or four different accounts in the same bank, you won't be charged a fee for going under the NOW account minimum.

Some banks still charge you an amount per check. It's up to you to shop around and determine whether the interest will outweigh the bank charges when you open a NOW account. NOW accounts are mainly for people who write a steady number of checks but can maintain a minimum checking account balance to receive interest.

Deluxe accounts, which are loaded with extra features such as free travelers checks and other services, are also offered, as are club accounts, which may be tied in with other bank services such as various discounts. Many banks offer self-service accounts that tie to an ATM to encourage ATM use. Basic checking accounts still exist, and for three or four dollars a month, they allow you to write about 10 checks. These lifeline accounts are good for people who have a limited need for a checking account.

Some banks also offer overdraft accounts. Be careful with these. If you spend more money than you have in your checking account, the bank will loan you the extra money to cover your expense. And they will do this every time. They will also charge a very high rate of interest for this feature. You then have to pay off the overdraft or carry an ongoing balance with high interest. You are better off simply keeping track of how much is in your checking account.

The ideal checking account is one that doesn't cost money to maintain, has a low minimum balance, allows you to write as many checks as necessary, pays interest, and provides you with up-to-date statements regularly.

Money Market Bank Deposit Accounts (MMDAs)

MMDAs came into existence in the mid 1980s because banks wanted to compete against mutual funds. Money market deposit accounts pay slightly higher interest rates than NOW or passbook savings accounts because they limit the number of checks, ATM withdrawals, or electronic transfers you are able to make to only three per month.

This is where banks can be very competitive, as they vary their rates depending on the overall state of interest rates. They may pay higher rates if you have more money invested in the account. On the other hand, they may charge bank fees if you drop below a certain minimum balance.

Money market deposit accounts are for people who want a liquid account, may want to write some checks, and want less risk than mutual funds. They are insured by the FDIC, which makes some people feel more comfortable. They are also part of your local bank, so you keep your money close to home. It's a no-risk, "higher level of comfort" account with check writing capabilities plus interest.

Certificates of Deposit (CDs)

CDs allow you to secure the same interest rate for a fixed amount of time, and the principal will not fluctuate. Through your bank, or a credit union, you can purchase CDs for three months, six months, one year, or longer. The longer you commit to with your CD, the higher your yield will be. On the other side of the equation is the early withdrawal penalty, should you need to cash in the CD before it is due. CDs are good short-term, no-risk places to invest money while you investigate your longer term plans. They are a way of playing it safe, particularly because they are insured by the FDIC.

Banks usually set a low minimum and do not charge for purchasing such a certificate. Interest rates will vary depending on the bank, the amount of money, and time frame you specify. Some banks even allow for designer CDs, which let you set the guidelines while the bank calculates the rate. Interest rate parameters are determined by the banks in conjunction with the demand and expected future demand for loans.

The annual percentage yield on your CD is what the CD will earn on an annual basis, combining the stated rate of interest and the compounded frequency. The annual yields generally run between 4 and 6 percent, depending on whether you purchase a six-month, one-year, or five-year CD. This is similar to short- and intermediate-term bonds. The interest from your CD is taxable.

U.S. Treasury Bills

Backed by the United States government, T-bills, as they are widely known, are safe purchases because there is no threat of losing the principal. More popular before the mutual fund wave of the '90s (T-bill interest rates reached double digits in the '80s), they are sold at government auctions (every Monday except bank holidays) and offered for 13, 26, or 52 weeks. Essentially, the government determines the rate of yield at the treasury auctions. This determines what yield you will receive when you buy the T-bill. Current T-bill rates are typically in the 5 to 5.5 percent range.

When you buy one, you immediately get a payment of interest (called the "discount"), and when the T-bill becomes due, you can reinvest and receive a discount payment again.

For example, let's say you buy a 26-week T-bill for $10,000. You then immediately receive a check for $300 (at an interest rate of around 6 percent) as your discount. Then, after the six months are up, you will receive another check for the original $10,000 you invested. Or you can renew it indefinitely.

Treasury bills are investments made with the federal government. Therefore, you can bypass your local bank and purchase them from any federal reserve bank or from the Bureau of Public Debt at the Treasury Department. The interest can then be routed directly into your bank account or money market account.

Anyone can buy Treasury bills in thousand dollar denominations starting as low as $1,000. For more information, contact the Bureau of Public Debt, Treasury Department, Washington, DC, 20239 or talk with a banker.

While T-bill interest payments are taxable at the federal level, they are not taxable at the state or local level, so if you reside in a state with high taxes, this might be an attractive investment. Also, the T-bill tax is paid when the bill becomes due. Thus, if you bought a six-month bill in June of 2001, the taxable income will not show up until 2002, and it will be reported on the return you submit in 2003.

How to Choose a Bank

Despite mergers and acquisitions, there are still over nine thousand banks operating in the United States—down from some fifteen thousand in the '80s. Indeed, you still have a great many banks to choose from.

Here's what to look for when choosing a bank:

- Check the interest rates, and if you need a loan or mortgage, check those rates as well.

    What does the bank offer? Some banks offer broker services. Others have free home money management software such as Intuit Quicken or Microsoft Money. Free checking is always nice, too. There are numerous services banks can now include.
- Determine the convenience of ATMs. Does the bank have accessibility to ATMs in other locations? Is there a surcharge for using the machines?
- Look at bank fees. For example, compare unlimited checks versus paying per check. Don't forget about account minimums.
- Does the bank offer online services? Do they have their own service, or do they use a commercial server? What do they charge for home banking?
- Look to see whether they have linking accounts, which are common today. This basically means that your minimum in one account may be lower than the allotted minimum, but because your balance is higher in another account and they are linked together, you will not be charged a minimum fee.
- Location and hours are always important.
- Visit the local branch and get to know the characteristics of that bank. What level of personal service would you like?
- And finally, how safe is your bank? Is it FDIC protected? Is it solvent? Do some research. You can check out the rating of a bank by calling Veribanc (1-800-44-BANKS). For a $10 fee, Veribanc will give you the bank's safety rating.

Balancing Your Checkbook

It is very important to balance your checking account at the end of every month. Doing so will help ensure that your account is never overdrawn and that the bank has not made any errors. It will also help you keep on top of your expenses and income.

It is very simple to keep your checkbook balanced. Most bank statements include instructions but, here are the basic steps you can follow:

1. Enter each check you write, including the date, check number, payee, and amount paid.
2. Deduct the amount paid from the account balance.
3. Enter each deposit including the date and amount.
4. Add the amount deposited to the account balance.
5. Be sure to deduct all ATM withdrawals (this is commonly forgotten).
6. Be sure to add in any direct deposits (paychecks, interest, etc.).
7. Be sure to deduct any bank charges or fees charged to your account.

When you receive your monthly statement, follow these steps:

1. Compare the canceled checks to the checks written since the previous statement.
2. Do the same for any deposits made.
3. Since it takes checks a few days to clear and you may have written some after your statement was sent to you, you should list all outstanding checks (including those written in prior months) so that your checkbook will balance with the statement. Keep track of these items so that you can see if they clear on your next statement.

Some people want to balance their checkbook to the penny. Others have neither the time nor the patience and are satisfied knowing that they have enough money to cover their check writing needs. The choice is yours.

Many personal organizers and check balancing computer programs can also be used as well. It depends on the volume of checks you write as to whether or not software is really necessary. Make sure you double check your entries. Hard copies are always nice, just in case of a technological glitch.

Online Banking

Nearly five million American households are doing their banking online. Why the sudden popularity of banking by computer?

The most appealing aspect of online banking is accessibility. You are no longer at the mercy of the bank statement arriving on time in the mail or of banking hours, and you can view your account whenever you choose. You'll be able to download statements, see that your checkbook is balanced, and pay bills whenever they come in—or program them to be paid on a particular date, from the comfort of your own home. And if paying bills online isn't enough technology for you, the next wave, e-billing, has already begun.

All you need to do is select a bank that has online banking accessibility and a platform or way of making the connection. Typically, Intuit Quicken, Microsoft Money, Managing Your Money, or, in some cases, America Online will provide you the access you need. You can also receive proprietary software from the bank. Some banks will only be found on the Internet, but most won't require you to be Internet users.

As is the case with all banking these days, when selecting an online bank, you need to look at the cost factor. While CitiBank offers both free online banking and bill paying, others offer free online banking but charge for bill paying at anywhere from $.50 per bill to $9.95 a month for twenty bills. The trick is to go online and shop around. Learn what your bank offers, what you can download, and what the costs will be. Find a bank that meets your needs at a cost that is right for you.

While there is still some concern over the safety of online banking, banks maintain a high level of confidence and stand behind online banking. In fact, online banking is so safe that most banks will not hold the customer responsible if a hacker gets in, which isn't to say there will not be an inconvenience. Choosing to do your banking online is most often based on the habits and computer comfort level of the individual.

chapter five

Stocks

Stocks are generally one of the very best investments you can make, especially if you can invest for a period of years. Despite the stock market's volatile nature over the past few years, it is still the place where many people are now sprucing up their portfolios. Intimidating to some, the market is accessible to people at all levels of income. However, because of the risk, it is not the place to invest if you do not have a cushion in a risk-free area. It is also not the place to invest if you are uncomfortable taking some level of risk.

Although buying low and selling high is the basic premise, there are variations on that theme. Numerous financial studies show that holding onto a stock for a longer period of time, such as five to 10 years, will reduce the risk of losing your money considerably. Over the long haul, stocks are a solid way of building your assets. However, you need to understand that some years the value of all U.S. stock markets have gone down. So no matter what stock you invest in, there will be some months, even a year or two, when the value of your investment actually decreases.

To increase your likelihood of holding onto winners, you might want to consider a mutual fund (a collection of stocks or bonds). A mutual fund diversifies your investmentthrough the purchase of several stocks, bonds, or sometimes a combination of both. Good fund managers balance more volatile stocks with those that have shown greater consistency. They compensate for one bad choice with several good ones. Although they can be wrong, and mutual funds have lost money, the majority of them in recent years have performed well, some showing over 30 to 40 percent in annual returns.

Stock Basics

A company sells shares of stock to help raise equity to operate and in turn, grow. They anticipate both growth and profits. Those profits will be reflected in the activity of the stock and those who have invested (own shares) will be along for the ride. The first time a company issues stock it is called an initial public offering (IPO). Companies that have issued stock previously offer what is called a primary offering when they offer new stock.

The detailed process of issuing stock is usually done through an investment bank, with whom the company works to determine how much capital is needed, what price they will sell the stock at, how much it will cost them to issue such equities, and so on. A company must file a registration statement with the Securities and Exchange Commission (SEC), which then carefully investigates whether the company has made full disclosure in compliance with the Securities Act of 1933. The SEC then determines whether the company has met all the criteria to issue common stock, or "go public."

When the stock is ready to be sold to the public, a price is issued in accordance with the current market. The best way for you to find out about an IPO is to get yourself a broker who has a pulse on all the late breaking financial news. Companies will often call the leading brokerage houses and brokers with whom they are familiar so that they can inform their clients about such an offering. They look for investors who will hold onto the stock for a long period of time. As is the case with anything new, these stocks are likely to be volatile at first and, thus, can be very risky. Sometimes it is best to wait and see where the stock eventually settles.

The vast majority of stocks have been on the market for some time. They fall into several categories including blue chip stocks, growth stocks, income stocks, and cyclical stocks.

Blue chip stock is issued by companies such as IBM, Procter & Gamble, and Disney. Such prestigious, established major companies have solid reputations in the market. Most have been around more than 25 years and show no signs of slowing down.

Cyclical stocks are those of companies whose earnings are most closely tied to the business cycle. As the economy fluctuates these stocks will move up or down along with it. Stocks in automobiles, such as General Motors, for example, will be cyclical because when the economy is bad, fewer people will buy new cars, and when the economy is good, car buying will be up. Companies that make products such as food, are not cyclical since food is a constant in any economy. Stocks for which there is a consistent demand, regardless of the economic climate, are non-cyclical.

Growth stocks, as the name suggests, are issued by companies that are looking to grow and expand. You may be on a roller-coaster ride with such a company at the outset, but if their prognosis is correct, they will grow successfully over a period of time. When personal computers and the Internet were just starting to catch on, companies offering new software and search engines were the hot ticket.

There are different varieties of income stocks. Many are considered safer stocks, or less of a risk. They pay steady dividends because frequently they are issued by long-time well-established companies, rather than by groundbreaking newcomers. Utility companies, for example, often fall into this category. Prices do vary, but income stocks usually compete with the bond market, where such steady income is similar. Stocks, however, can pay a higher rate—plus the stock can go up—whereas the bond principal remains the same. Many older stocks also pay dividends, which may make them appear more attractive to buyers. These, too, are often considered to be less risky stocks.

The bottom line is that there are numerous types of common (anyone can buy) stocks, but they all perform in the same manner. You buy them low and hope and pray that they go up! Evaluate the company you are looking to buy shares of and try to determine the outlook for their future, based on their past track record, their current stability, and their future plans and goals.

Preferred stocks also need to increase in value for you, the investor to make money. They are somewhat like bonds in that they have a fixed dividend rate, payable every month or quarter. Most often these are offered by long-time stable companies. Preferred stocks are usually less volatile than common stocks. Also, companies pay preferred stock dividends before they pay common stock dividends. Some are even dubbed convertible stocks, meaning they can be converted into shares of common stocks.

Stocks and You

When you buy shares of stock, you essentially become one of many investors in that company. A public company allows the public to become owners, or have equity, in the company. Stocks are, therefore, also known as equities. The price of the stock depends on how many shares have been sold. If the future of the company looks promising, then the stock becomes sought after and the price rises. Conversely, if the company experiences a downswing, shareholders sell and the price drops. Thus, your shares increase and decrease in value based on the buying and selling, or trading, of the shares of stock in the company.

As a shareholder of stock, you receive quarterly and annual reports detailing the history of the business, the major players, and the earnings of the company. Also, ownership of a common stock gives you voting rights, usually at one vote per share owned. Although you may enjoy having a say in company matters, the reality is that the major shareholders determine the direction the company will take. However, you are entitled to go to stockholders' meetings, if you so choose, to learn more about the direction the company is taking.

Stocks are purchased at the current price per share listed for that stock. For example, 100 shares of XYZ, listed at 20 on the exchange, would cost $2,000. Selling those same shares at 27 would bring you $2,700, or a $700 profit. Those are the bare basics.

Unlike other investments, where there may be a binding time agreement (e.g., a retirement plan, from which you cannot withdraw money until you reach a certain age), you can hold onto stocks for as long as you choose, from several days to many years (unless, of course, the company goes out of business). Shares of stock can be willed, given through a trust, or gifted to another person. Shares of stock received by an heir to an estate are not taxable to the heir upon receipt, but a capital gains tax may have to be paid when the shares are sold.

Choosing Stocks

If you're going to buy shares of stock, it's to your benefit to do some homework. First, you should know something about the company you are investing in. Look at their annual report, look them up online, and find articles that talk about their future plans. To keep up with day-to-day stock market activities, check your local newspapers, *USA Today*, or the *Wall Street Journal*, if you want more detailed information. You can also tune in to CNN, FNN, or other financial radio or television networks. Nearly every company now has its own Web site, as do financial newspapers, magazines, and various information services.

Companies file annual reports, quarterly reports, special reports, proxy statements, and various other information with the Securities and Exchange Commission (SEC). You can look up reports at the SEC's public reference rooms in Washington, DC, New York City, and Chicago. The SEC has a Web site at *www.sec.gov*. The address of the SEC is U.S. Securities and Exchange Commission, 450 5th Street NW, Washington, DC, 20549.

For many people, the best company to invest in is one that they are familiar with in their daily lives. If you are a pharmacist, for example, and you know a new drug is flying off the shelf, you might invest in that pharmaceutical company, after reading up on it of course. Likewise, if there is a product you are reading about for your own needs or items you find yourself becoming more familiar with for your children, these may be the companies to look up, since you are already familiar with their product.

You also need not dive in with a huge investment. Start slowly, get the feel for following the market, and then buy more. It's a good idea to diversify (which is why mutual funds are so incredibly popular).

Stock Market Indicators

The leading indicator of the stock market for over 100 years has been the Dow Jones Industrial Average, which is considered the most significant pillar of American capitalism. The Dow represents thirty blue chip industrials, plus transportation and utility components. Occasionally these companies change, however, many of these companies are staples in American business, which explains why when the Dow drops, investors are concerned. While your biggest concern is not the Dow as a whole but the individual stocks within it that you own, the Dow does act as a good barometer of the overall market.

The S&P (Standard & Poor's) 500 index is also a leading player in the business of evaluating, analyzing, and disseminating market information. Widely respected because of their in-depth coverage of the market, the S&P 500 has become the standard by which experts judge their success at selecting stocks and mutual funds. Few actually beat the S&P index (although many claim to).

Another leading stock market indicator is the NASDAQ Composite Index. The NASDAQ includes over 5,000 companies, which is more than most indexes. Because it has such a broad base, the NASDAQ Composite Index has become increasingly popular. It is market-value weighted, which means that each company listed will affect the index in proportion to its market value.

Buying Stocks

If you are comfortable with picking stocks, have done your homework, and feel confident that you know what you are doing, you can call a discount broker, buy stocks directly from the company, or buy stocks online. If you are looking for more guidance, want more detailed reports, and seek advice, you can go to a full-service broker. Full service, as the term implies, will provide you with more information and recommendations. In some cases a full-service broker can buy and sell for you on his or her own (at your discretion, of course). Naturally, a full-service broker takes a higher commission.

When signing up with a brokerage firm, you will receive a new account agreement. Look over the agreement carefully before signing. There are a few decisions you will be asked to make regarding an account with a brokerage firm.

First you must determine who will have the decision-making capacity regarding the account. Does the representative have discretionary authority to make decisions for you? This is up to you and usually not advised until you are very comfortable with the broker. Advice and discretionary authority are not the same thing. Also, can anyone else contact the broker on your account? Your spouse? Your son or daughter? (Account agreements with online brokerage firms will be slightly different since you essentially play the role of the broker. Online trading will be discussed in greater detail later in the chapter.)

Another decision involves how you will pay for your investments. It is common to maintain a cash account in which you can pay for each transaction as it is made. A margin account allows you to borrow money from the brokerage house to buy securities. You then pay interest on the account. Margin accounts can be dangerous, because if the loan becomes greater than the value of the stock, you are liable for the balance. Essentially, you are playing with borrowed money.

Keep in mind that because the stock market is like a living organism, it keeps on moving. Therefore, if you call to buy a stock at 23, it could be 22 ⅞ or 23 ¼ when the broker is actually able to purchase it or sell it for you. When purchasing, you can set a limit and say to the broker, for example, "If it's over 23 ½, don't purchase it." Besides a limit order to buy or sell at a specific price or better, you can also place a stop limit order, which becomes an order to buy as soon as a trade occurs at the target price. Conversely, a sell stop limit means that as soon as a stock reaches a certain target price, or drops to a certain price, it is to be sold. There are various other orders you can place, such as a day order to be placed that day only.

Care to Drip or Dip?

Dividend Reinvestment Plans (or DRPs, sometimes called Drips) and Dividend Investment Plans (DIPs) are plans in which you can purchase stock directly from a company. The plan essentially has you starting with a small amount of money and reinvesting it as you receive dividends. It is a way of starting small and letting your money buy more shares as it grows through dividends. It is almost like a stock bank account, except the results should be much better over time.

Another nice feature about a DRP, besides allowing you to start off small, is that you can buy stock consistently without having to do anything. In most cases you can add to the amount by purchasing more shares if you choose. Otherwise, you can let the dividend reinvestment grow into substantial capital on its own.

Although you can often purchase a DRP or DIP directly from the company, you can also go to a transfer agent such as Chase Mellon or Boston Equiserve. They can provide you with more options while making it easier in terms of paperwork and administration for the company. Since they are hired by the company, you are not charged a fee.

Other Considerations When Buying Stocks

1. Don't believe everything you read. Many hot tips have gone askew over the years. Take all "can't miss" candidates with a grain of salt and do your own research.

2. Avoid peer pressure. Don't get suckered into buying or selling because everyone else says you should. Listen to what others say but make your own determination.

3. Determine whether you need a full-service stock broker or a discount broker.

4. Save the business section. From the *Wall Street Journal* to FNN to *USA Today*, there are numerous ways to follow the stock market. Make a habit of checking up on your stocks on a daily basis. Most online services provide easy access to the day's stock prices, with many providing information about the company as well.

5. Do some bargain hunting. Keep an eye on stocks that don't appear to be doing well at present but may be heading for a rebound. These can be good purchases. You need to find a valid reason why a stock may go back up, such as some new technology, forthcoming product, merger, or acquisition.

6. Get a second opinion. You should double check a recommended stock with someone whose financial knowledge and opinion you respect.
7. Keep the word risk in mind. Don't let it scare you, but remember that stocks promising greater short-term rates of return are also riskier, meaning your chance of losing money is also greater.
8. Pay attention to any announcements, such as information about a stock split, made by the company you own stock in. Mergers, buyouts, reorganizations, third-party actions, and other factors can affect your investments. Read any such notices or announcements carefully.
9. Insider trading does exist. Be wary of any recommendation from an "inside source" regarding any confidential information, a prospective merger, a new product, and so on.
10. Stay within your limit. If you have set aside $10,000 for the stock market and your stock has risen by 5 points, it's not uncommon to invest the profits, if you choose. On the other hand, if you've lost money, don't beg, borrow, or steal another $10,000 to reinvest.

All in all, the market is the place to be right now if you have money to invest and can handle some level of risk. However, it is not the only place to be. Don't put all your money in the market, no matter how good it looks.

Choosing a Broker or Brokerage House

There are a number of factors you need to consider when determining which broker or brokerage house will handle your transactions. It's worth your time to evaluate any dealer of securities before putting your confidence in one to handle your account. First and foremost, you need to determine whether to go with a full-service broker or a discount brokerage house. They both have access to the same stocks; the difference is in how much advice, input, and service you want.

Prior to consulting a broker, determine your financial goals and objectives. It's important to know what you are looking for and to determine your level of risk. It is also important to have a solid idea of your current financial situation.

When evaluating brokers, get answers to these questions:

- What is the sales background and experience of the broker?
- What is the history of the firm or brokerage house?
- How much are the commissions? Commissions vary widely, depending on whether you are using a discount or full-service broker. Also factored heavily into the equation are the number of shares you are buying and the price per share.
- What fees will you have to pay when opening, maintaining, or closing an account?
- Is the brokerage firm a member of the Securities Investor Protection Corporation? SIPC can help consumers to some degree if the firm goes bankrupt. Ask if the firm has other insurance.
- Are the account representatives accessible? Who covers for them?
- If you're dealing with a full-service brokerage house, what services do they provide and what is their market strategy and philosophy?

The National Association of Securities Dealers can answer your questions and alleviate your concerns about the practices of a particular dealer or look up his or her past record regarding any disciplinary actions taken or complaints registered. They can also let you know if the broker is licensed to do business in your state. (Call NASD at 800/289-9999.) You can also inquire or register a complaint about a broker or brokerage house by contacting the SEC Office of Consumer Affairs at 202/942-7040.

Online Trading

If you feel you are comfortable enough with the stock market to make decisions without the aid of a broker, you may consider buying stocks online. Your computer will connect you directly with the brokerage house; no longer will you have to wait by the phone for the broker to return your call.

It is rather easy to set up an account with an online brokerage firm. Most allow you to fill out the necessary forms electronically. Be prepared to give your full name and address, as well as social security number and employer information. If you do not feel secure sending this information via the Internet, you can also print out the forms and mail or fax them to the brokerage firm. However, keep in mind that by doing this, you cause a delay in accessing your account. The minimum amount required to open an account varies between firms, though generally the minimum will not fall less than $2,000.

There are several advantages to online trading. Normally, it is cheaper and faster to trade online as compared to going through a broker. Online brokerage firms also give you access to a variety of products and services to help you manage your investments. Real-time quotes, stock charts, company profiles, market summaries, and 24-hour customer service are a few of the amenities most online brokerages offer.

A lot of people are using online trading as a way of expediting their transactions. Online trading allows you to make transactions day and night. However, before you jump at this new techno-trading possibility, there are a few things to consider.

The idea of quick trading and easy access lends itself to short-term wheeling and dealing. After all, if you are going to hold the bulk of your stocks for five to 10 years, occasionally buying or selling a few shares, why not just have a discount broker you can call? Therefore, it is important that you assess your reason for online trading. Are you playing the market on a short-term basis? And, if so, will you abuse the new trading technology? The problem (as with credit cards, off-track betting, and other means of easy spending) is that people tend to overdo it. Online trading opens up a can of worms for people who are impulsive. It can make trading too easy.

Ask a few computer-related questions. If your system is down and you are unable to get online or the site itself is down, what do you do as your stock plummets or your hot up-and-comer becomes everyone's hot up-and-comer? Make sure there is an alternative way of reaching the online broker and getting whatever information you need.

Also keep in mind that with online trading you will not receive the advice that you would get from a broker. Because you don't have all the information and expertise a traditional broker has, it is important to carefully review all possible transactions. Don't get too caught up in the fast-paced world of online buying and trading. Do your homework and make educated trades.

The major online brokerage firms are Ameritrade (*www.ameritrade.com*), E*Trade (*www.etrade.com*), Charles Schwab (*www.schwab.com*), and TD Waterhouse Group (*www.tdwaterhousegroup.com*). Each of these firms will give you additional information, as well as take you step by step through the online trading process.

Though online trading makes playing the stock market quick and easy, don't forget that paperwork is important. You should keep records of all transactions. Make sure you can and do obtain them.

Systems and Strategies

There are numerous systems and strategies to playing the market, but the only one that works is the one in which you come out ahead. Dollar cost averaging is very popular. Essentially you invest x amount of dollars into a stock on a regular weekly, monthly, or bimonthly basis. This allows you to buy more shares when the stock goes down and less when the stock is high, which is where the averaging comes from.

For this system to work well, it is important for you to invest consistently. It is also recommended that you do so with a few stocks (around four or five) at one time, which means your winners will balance out your losers. You'll be able to hang onto what appear to be losers for a longer time because you will have other stocks balancing them out. Essentially, buying several stocks and creating your own portfolio is akin to creating your own personal mutual fund. However, you are the portfolio manager.

Not unlike mutual funds, it is advantageous to invest in several industry groups. The market is broken into a number of groups. Some of the more timely industries include:

- Health care
- Home building
- Manufacturing, recreational vehicles
- Air transport
- Computer software and services
- Financial services

- Home furnishings
- Retail building supplies
- Office equipment and supplies
- Advertising
- Environmental
- Restaurant
- Industrial
- Cable television
- Retail stores
- Telecommunications equipment

Some of the less timely industries include the following:

- Copper
- Metals and mining
- Paper and forest products
- Petroleum
- Steel
- Shoe manufacturing
- Natural gas
- Publishing
- Electrical equipment
- Coal/alternate energy
- Machinery

If you read that an industry may be on the rebound, you might take a risk while holding onto stocks in more timely industries in your portfolio. Watch for changing trends. You may also diversify between high-cap and low-cap stocks, that is, larger and smaller companies. You might have a few Dow Jones blue-chippers paying dividends and a couple of more volatile new high-growth, high-risk stocks in emerging young companies. Balance is important in a portfolio.

Another way to maximize your investments is to look up the 52-week high and low for a stock (easily located online or in any number of stock market programs or in the financial section of a paper). The high and low give you a good indication of the parameters of this stock. Assuming you have read about and feel comfortable with the company, look to purchase this stock when it is as close to its 52-week low as possible. One way to do that is to use "open orders" to have the stock bought at the price you want it. Therefore, if the stock does not drop to that price, you don't purchase it. This plan is more effective if you choose several stocks at very low prices, it's likely that two or three will reach the price at which you are looking to buy them. This takes patience; but you'll have several stocks selected at very low prices over the course of six, 12, or 18 months.

Some advisors suggest that you start with bigger, large-cap stocks; then once they've gone up, sell some of the shares and play with your profit by putting it into small- or mid-cap stocks, which traditionally perform well, but can be more risky. You also need to make your selections more carefully. While your money grows over time in the large-cap stocks, you can follow the smaller- and medium-sized companies to determine what you will buy once you sell off some of your shares.

There are many other systems you can use. Some have you reinvesting the profits into other areas, such as bonds; others have you planning to sell off each stock once it reaches a certain level or percentage gained. The bottom line is to pick a strategy that works for you and stick with it.

chapter six

Mutual Funds

Mutual funds offer a way to play the stock market without having to pick individual stocks. They have also evolved into a way to invest in bonds or in cash vehicles without having to carefully select those either. In fact, one of the advantages of a mutual fund company is that experts make selections for you. The other advantage is diversification. It's the "don't put all your eggs in one basket" theory that makes mutual funds so attractive and so successful.

There are thousands of mutual funds to choose from to suit all investment needs. Magazines and newspapers such as *Money*, *Kiplingers*, *Forbes*, and the *Wall Street Journal* keep you apprised of the hottest ones. Online services at a wide variety of sites can also update you on the latest mutual funds, with fund companies offering their own Web services.

Choose a fund according to your own situation and preferences as well as the historical performance of the fund and the outlook for the future. As a shrewd fund shopper you should evaluate the level of risk and assess the background of the fund manager. Naturally, the more you invest and the more risky the investment (such as a short-term aggressive-growth equity fund), the more carefully you need to select. Once you determine the type of fund for you, the next step is to shop for the best returns.

Mutual funds diversify your money for you. The manager must try to meet the goal of the fund, be it income in steady yields or growth. The risk factor depends on the type of fund. Low-risk funds provide a steady interest level but do not offer the growth potential of higher-risk funds, which obviously take a bigger gamble with your money. All securities purchased by the fund are pooled and owned mutually by the fund's investors, and comprise the portfolio of that fund. Shareholders are paid based on the number of shares they own and the performance of the overall portfolio.

One item to consider when reviewing several competitive funds is operating expenses. Operating expenses, or expense ratios, generally run in the .70 to 1.50 percent range. This is one reason why mutual fund companies hold over $4 trillion in assets. It is also part of the calculating that you need to do to determine which fund is really better for you. Better yields are not really better if you are paying too much in expenses for fund management.

Risk Versus Reward and Risk Versus Tolerance

Base your determination of risk on how much you can afford to invest and what your goals are. Money market and fixed income mutual funds are in the low-risk category; growth and aggressive growth stock funds are in the higher-risk category. If you are just starting to save money for college tuition or retirement, with years ahead of you, you might decide on aggressive growth to build up your assets. If you are nearing retirement age or have a child going off to college, you might decide to play it much safer and choose low-risk funds.

Unlike the idea of risk/reward, which means that you take a risk in order to achieve a potential reward, risk/tolerance refers to how much risk you feel comfortable taking. It is a part of your personality that plays a major role in your investing strategies. In fact, it generally is the first question asked by a financial planner.

There are individuals who will jump at the chance to make money now and others who are content letting money accrue over time. There are many people that fall somewhere in between. Just as market volatility measures mutual funds, tolerance measures your own personal "volatility" level.

Some people are comfortable earning a safe 6 percent on an investment they know about and trust, and do not have to monitor carefully; others are willing to take a risk for a possible 15 percent return on their investment. It's up to you.

Mutual fund minimum investments range dramatically, with most being between $250 and $10,000. There are some at $100 and others at $25,000. Stay in your comfort zone.

The other part of doing your fund homework in the world of investments is determining the risk versus reward factor. One of the reasons the country has embraced mutuals so strongly in recent years is because they offer both ends of the spectrum and everything in between. There is something exciting, for many people, about taking some level of risk in hopes of financial reward. Your acceptance of risk versus reward, or how liberal or conservative you are, should be the determining factor.

Funds always have some level of risk attached. But the risk is lower in short-term bond funds and much higher in junk bond and stock funds, especially for the short term.

Stock Funds

Stock funds are the most common types of mutual funds available. They are also probably the most exciting type and certainly the most active. Based on the volatility of the market, stock funds buy and sell stocks with your money. It is important, therefore, that you "play the market" through the hands of a skilled portfolio manager and that you have several stocks earning you money.

Like all mutual fund groups, stock funds have a variety of options: aggressive growth, long-term growth, growth and income, balanced, international general, international regional, global, sector. Aggressive growth funds are the most volatile. The idea of short-term growth in the market is the most risky category and, therefore, where you need to be the most careful when making a selection of a fund and fund manager.

Long-term growth stock funds are slightly safer; you still deal with the market, but you play in a longer time frame. The longer you stay in the market, the less risk you are taking. The one-year best and worst performances since 1926 range from a +54 percent to a -43 percent; the five-year difference is +24 percent to -13 percent; and the 15-year difference is +20 percent to +1 percent. Therefore, if you want to play more conservatively, you might be better with a long-term fund. These funds are often advisable for retirement planning. Stocks in these funds are proven to be slow but steady.

There are also growth and income funds that offer a little of each. They are less volatile because the portfolio is balanced between stocks that will perform best over a long term and provide dividends, and stocks that will fluctuate and be bought and sold by the fund manager on a short-term basis.

International stock funds are risky. In recent years, the international market has not been strong, so be cautious.

Bond Funds

Bond funds provide steady interest because they invest in fixed income securities. The yields are usually a little higher than money market mutual funds but also a little more risky. If interest rates increase, the value of the bond fund can decrease, thus creating a greater risk to you. However, that depends on the type of bonds.

There are a host of bond funds to choose from (investment grade, high-yield corporate, international, mortgage securities, investment grade munis, high-yield munis) that buy either short- or long-term bonds. Bond high-yield funds, for example, buy current high-yield bonds, also known as junk bonds. International bond funds buy bonds issued by governments and corporations around the world. Other funds buy short-, intermediate-, and long-term bonds. One of the advantages of bond funds over buying bonds individually is that when bond interest is paid, you may not be able to buy another bond, should you choose to, but instead have to funnel the interest into a money market account until you have enough to buy a bond. With a bond fund, you can have your dividends reinvested automatically. Also, bond fund managers are experts, or should be.

Last, but certainly not least, is the opportunity to buy tax-free funds if you are in a high tax bracket. These will pay a lower yield, but if you are in a high tax bracket or are living in a state or city with high taxes, you might benefit from the lesser yield. It may be to your advantage to make some dividend comparisons between taxable and tax-free funds. Tax-free bond funds are offered by most major fund companies.

Money Market Mutual Funds

Money market mutual funds (not to be confused with money market deposit accounts) are popular investment vehicles offering steady yields. They are offered by fund management companies who invest in high-quality short-term investments, such as CDs and bankers' acceptances, and return a yield after deducting their operating expenses. They are share-based, which means they offer a rate of $1 per one share, and, therefore, a low-risk option. Generally, they offer check writing privileges and let you sell off shares when you choose (the money is wired into your bank account or sent by check to your home).

Money market mutual funds are fashionable because they offer a lot of the positives that most people are seeking in their investments. Due to the competition brought on by the influx of so many fund companies, the yields are higher than bank interest, usually in the 4 to 6 percent range. They are for anyone who wants to maintain a low risk, earn primarily interest income, and have easy access to their money. In higher tax brackets, you can get a tax-free money market account, at a lower yield. Because they retain a constant $1 per share price, the seven-day yield is the best way to follow money market fund performance.

Balanced Funds

Balanced funds invest in both stocks and bonds. This allows them the best of both worlds, paying high dividends and reaping the long-term growth benefits of stocks. A good fund manager will be able to keep the appropriate balance by moving the majority of the fund revenues into bonds or cash instruments when necessary. Conversely, if the market is on the rise, the manager can invest more heavily in it.

Load Versus No-Load Funds

The difference between load and no-load funds has to do with the method by which they are purchased. Load funds are purchased through a salesperson, to whom you pay a commission. No-load funds are purchased by you directly, often through a toll-free number. How you purchase a fund depends primarily on how much time you have to do your mutual fund homework and how comfortable you are in your knowledge of funds. Between books, magazines, financial programs on radio and television, the financial network, and the Internet, there is a wealth of information out there from which you can make your own determinations. However, there are salespeople trained in the area of mutual funds who have expertise that is not easily acquired. They can save you time and give you pointers.

You can now get middle-of-the-road funds. These "loaded no-loads" have catches to them, however, in that somewhere along the line you pay extra. For example, you may pay extra for selecting a no-load fund from a catalog or pay a $500 fee for a "personal finance report." You need to consider whether you are defeating the purpose of a no-load fund when paying any extra costs for a loaded no-load. There are also back-end loads, which charge you a fee if you sell the fund within the first several years of owning it. The longer you own it, the smaller the fee.

Since many mutual fund purchases are made through toll-free numbers, you can shop around for funds all over the country. The *Wall Street Journal*, *Kiplingers*, and other financial publications routinely list the best funds at any given time. The Money Fund Report from IBC in Ashland, Massachusetts (800/343-5413), keeps track of some 850 money market mutual funds, noting their seven-day yield, the companies' assets, and more. Companies with larger assets generally pass lower expenses on to you.

Read the Prospectus

You should read the prospectus before buying the fund, not to mention the leading up-to-date reports in the top financial magazines and in the many top-selling investment books.

The prospectus accompanies your fund application form, as mandated by the Securities and Exchange Commission. It explains the fund's goal—for example, to achieve steady income, income/growth, aggressive growth, and so forth—and how successful it has been over the last several years. It also apprises you of what types of stocks (or bonds) the fund purchases and gives you a breakdown. The prospectus tells you about the type of risk the fund takes, the background track-record information on the fund, the fees, whether the fund is taxed, the minimum investment allowed, whether you can reinvest dividends, and so on.

A typical prospectus tells you the number of years the company has been around. It also defines the type of fund and the goals, the fund performance over the past one, three, five, and/or 10 years, and the yield generated (if appropriate) over a given period of time. Consider, however, that the past performance is only a guide and cannot assure you of future performance. Yields change daily, based on rising and falling interest rates, market conditions, and the response to other factors such as political and economical events.

The prospectus should answer all your questions about a fund. The magazines and books will tell you how that fund rates in regard to other funds, and the experts will tell you what they foresee that fund doing in the future. Once you've covered these bases, you've done your homework.

So Many to Choose From

Choosing the right fund can be a gargantuan task, with nearly ten thousand mutual funds of varying types in an oversaturated marketplace. So, what do you do?

First, determine your personal goals, based on your assets, income/expenses, and needs. Are you saving for retirement? Are you putting away money for college tuition? Did you just collect $25,000 above and beyond your budget from an inheritance and want to get some rapid growth on this new-found money? It is important to assess and evaluate your own situation to eliminate the funds that don't fall into the category in which you are looking to invest.

Most major fund companies offer a wide range of funds to meet the needs of any type of investor, from conservative newcomers to seasoned aggressive investors who already know their way through the jungle of funds available. Talk with other people you know who have invested in a particular fund and find out why. Talk to several professionals who analyze funds and read the top magazines. *Money* magazine, for example, lists their top 100 funds for each year. It's a good starting point.

The bottom line is that you are looking for a fund that has a well-planned, clearly-defined strategy that meets your needs, has low expenses, has performed well, and is run by a manager you feel has a solid track record.

Keeping Track

National and local newspapers, along with financial networks and online services, can keep you abreast of your fund's current value. The net asset value (NAV) is the current price per share of the fund. To obtain the current value of your fund, multiply the number of shares by the price. Then compare this to the price at which you bought the fund.

	OBJ	NAV	WK	YTD	Retn./rank 4-yr
Mutual Fund Tables					
Fidelity Invest: MP		19.24	-.12	+5.6	+13.7/D
AMgr n					

What does it all mean? It's actually fairly simple. First, you have the name of the fund family and the specific fund. The OBJ, or objective, is the type of fund; in this case MP means mixed portfolio (a key accompanies the listings; it defines the various funds, such as CA for capital appreciation, SB for short-term bond fund, etc.). As mentioned above, the NAV, net asset value, is the current price at which you buy or sell shares of the fund. Then you have the movement of the fund by week (WK), year to date (YTD), and over four years; the final letter shows the fund's ranking versus other funds in the same objective category (some show 3- or 5-year returns).

You will often see what's called a Down Market category. This is not meant to discourage you but to reassure you that the better funds suffer less when the market goes bad. The number in that category gives you an idea of how the fund performed during tough times. Keep in mind that the income yield (how well the fund did to that point) is also factored in, so the decline is actually a little greater in most cases.

A volatility ranking tells you how much of a roller-coaster ride you can expect. Usually, it's a 1-to-10 ranking with ten fluctuating the most and one being the most stable.

Fund Managers

If someone is handling your money for you, it's important that you know something about this individual. Computers do not pick the funds; they only assist in generating the information and calculating the numbers. A good fund manager needs to have a proven track record over a period of several years. You should know the strategy of the fund manager and what type of stocks or bonds he or she specializes in buying.

Some managers take a more conservative approach, some try to keep expense costs lower, some do the bulk of stock selection themselves, and others work through numerous analysts. The bottom line is that you need to have confidence in the fund manager, so review his or her background carefully. Don't be dazzled by a young "hot" rookie fund manager who had one great year; it may have been a fluke. Look for managers with successful backgrounds. See how they fared in recent down markets. See how their fund companies rebounded and how their funds rate in the various money magazines. If a fund has changed managers often, that's not usually a good sign. Likewise, if a fund manager is at the helm of a different fund every year, that may not be reassuring either. Seek out consistency when dealing with investments. After all it's your money that's being played with!

chapter seven

Bonds

The bond market is not glamorous, but it is a relatively conservative way to watch your money grow. Although you never hear of bonds paying returns of 30 percent, high-rated bonds and government bonds are a very safe investment.

A bond is, essentially, a loan from you to a company or to the government. They are sold in specific increments and pay interest. When buying a bond, you can purchase it at face value, at a discount, or at a premium, depending on the interest rate of the bond and the interest rates of the market. The maturity date of the bond determines when you get your principal back. Bonds can be "called" earlier, which means the lender pays you back at an earlier date (as stated in the terms of the bond). You usually receive a premium, which is a little something extra for your troubles. A bond is usually called because the interest rate has dropped and the company wants to issue bonds at the lower rate.

If the company does very well, unlike with a stock, you will not benefit. Basically, with a bond, it's as though you lent $100 to someone who promised to pay back $125 over the next year. If, in the meantime, the person wins the lottery and has an additional $2 million, he or she still pays you $125 over the next year. If, on the other hand, the person's financial state is slightly worse, you still get your $125.

The wide variety of bonds has grown over the past 25 years and includes everything from municipal bonds to asset backed securities, zero coupon, and junk bonds. There are also bond mutual funds and combined equity/bond funds.

Before looking at the various types of bonds, it may be worth learning a little more about bonds themselves. First, bond prices vary in contrast to the interest rate. If interest rates rise above the rate at which you bought your bond, then your bond decreases in value. If interest rates drop, your bond is worth more. For example, if you buy a bond at 8 percent and the interest rate drops, the bond's value would increase—the 8 percent bond would be more valuable than bonds currently paying the lower rate—and vice versa. If you buy a bond at 8 percent and the interest rate rises to 10 percent, your 8 percent bond would not be as valuable as those bonds currently paying the higher interest rate.

Short-term bonds over the past 50 years have brought in average returns of over 4.5 percent; long-term bonds have brought in returns of around 6 percent. While these statistics may not be as dramatic as those of equity funds, it is a steady rate of return over a long period of time.

Calculate bond interest in terms of $1,000. If the yield is 7.5 percent, then you will receive $75 per each $1,000 you invest. In other words, a bond that pays $75 has a 7.5 percent yield. Most bonds have a set or fixed interest rate, but some have a "floating" rate, which means that the interest can change over time.

Types of Bonds

Bonds fall into several categories. Like all other investments, these categories vary in degree of risk. With any category of bonds, particularly long-term bonds, you have some degree of interest rate risk (rate fluctuations make the bond more or less valuable). The different bond categories center primarily around credit risk and yield. Naturally, the riskier bonds also provide the higher yield.

Categories of bonds run the gamut from Treasury bonds, which are essentially risk free, to bonds with government affiliated agencies like Fannie Mae and Ginnie Mae, to municipals, to investment grade corporate, and, finally, to the riskier junk bonds. Before choosing a category, evaluate your goals. Next, decide how much of your portfolio you plan to invest in bonds. Then, look at how much of a risk you are willing to take.

Government Bonds

U.S. government bonds are safe and solid investments. You do not pay state taxes, the bonds are backed by the United States government, and you can buy them directly from the Treasury Department without paying broker fees. (For more information, contact the Bureau of Public Debt, Division of Customer Services, Washington, DC 20239, 202/874-4000). By laddering, or staggering, several bonds with different maturities, you'll have money coming in consistently over a period of time.

Treasury bonds have maturity dates in excess of 10 years, with a minimum denomination of $1,000. Interest is paid on a semi-annual basis at a rate that varies with each issue. Treasury notes can have shorter maturity dates of two to ten years. Depending on the issue, the minimum investment ranges from $1,000 to $5,000.

Zero coupon bonds (also known as CATS, TIGERS, and LIONS) do not pay interest until the bond reaches maturity. The rate is higher, but you need to be patient. These bonds are good for a major future expenditure such as for a home or college tuition. Staggering four zeros to mature in each of the four years of college is a good laddered approach to help fund higher education.

In the area of savings bonds, EE savings bonds are issued at half their face value (or par value). Therefore, a $1,000 bond (face value) is purchased at $500. Interest accrues on the bond over a period of time. Series HH bonds, meanwhile, are interest paying bonds that mature in 10 years. Savings bonds can be had in denominations ranging from $25 to $10,000.

Mortgage-backed bonds often come from the Government National Mortgage Association (the GNMA, or Ginnie Mae) or the two housing corporations that are not officially part of the government but play a large role in home mortgage secondary lending, Fannie Mae and Freddie Mac. These organizations sell bonds that result from the purchase of numerous mortgages from either government agencies or lenders all across the country. Essentially, your bond is in the home mortgage field. Government agency bonds are also issued (in nonmortgage areas) by Sallie Mae (the Student Loan Marketing Association) and other federal agencies including the United States Postal Service.

Municipal Bonds

Also known as munis, municipal bonds are always popular as part of a diverse portfolio. Municipal bonds are issued by states, cities, counties, and local governments. They're not always graded (or rated), but when they are, they are almost always investment grade, particularly when secured. Yields are not generally high, but they are usually free of federal taxes. They are also usually free of state and local taxes—if issued by the state in which you reside. Therefore, you can accept a slightly lower yield if necessary.

Corporate Bonds

Corporations issue bonds to raise capital. They offer a host of different bonds, all of which are graded on the ability of the company to repay the bond holders. Among the various types of corporate bonds are convertible bonds, which can be converted into shares of stock in the issuing company (either on request or after a fixed time frame), and the risky high-yield junk bonds.

Yields on corporate bonds are paid semi-annually. Like stocks, corporate bonds are traded frequently. Trading is based on the price of the bond, which can fluctuate as a result of the company's financial outlook.

It's important to carefully study the company issuing the bond. Fortunately for most of us, bonds are rated. These ratings provide a significant indication of whether the company will default on the bonds.

Junk Bonds

Small companies, or those in shaky financial straits, may sell what are known as high-yield bonds, or more commonly, junk bonds. They are often new companies trying to raise money to establish themselves or companies in trouble looking to re-establish themselves. Junk bonds offer a high yield but are a major risk because of their greater chance of default (they do not receive investment grade ratings). Among several other downfalls of junk bonds is that they can be called when the company's financial picture improves, and the company can issue bonds at a lower interest rates. There is also the chance that the bond can be downgraded from a low rating to an even lower rating, causing the bond's price to drop. Be very careful with junk bonds—unless you are skilled in the bond trading market or have a diversified portfolio that can handle a junk bond or two.

Bond Ratings

Bonds are not uniformly rated. Like everything else, there are numerous types of ratings for bonds. Depending on the rating system used, the higher the rating, the better the bond, in terms of investment security. The more secure the bond, the easier it is to sell and the safer it is to own. Ratings are important with corporate bonds and sometimes with municipals; U.S. government bonds are secure.

Investment grade bonds are the highest rated bonds. Bonds issued by long-time stable corporations are usually rated higher because they are more secure, though not always.

Two of the most widely regarded rating systems are Standard & Poor's and Moody's. Standard & Poor's system runs as follows: AAA (highest rating), AA, A, BBB, BB, B, CCC, CC, C, and D. BB and BBB are the mid range—the lowest grade considered a reasonable investment. Anything in the C and D ratings have a high rate of default.

Moody's has a similar rating system: Aaa (highest), Aa, A, Baa, Ba, B, Caa, Ca, and C. Despite a penchant for the letter a, the system is similar to Standard & Poor's, with Baa and Ba ratings being the medium range, investment-grade bonds.

chapter eight

Retirement and Estate Planning

Social Security

Before venturing into the various ways in which you can set up retirement plans, it might be worth taking a quick look at the plan that the government has set up for you—the infamous Social Security.

Created to ensure that seniors were taken care of following the Great Depression, Social Security is relatively simple to understand. The FICA payment deducted from your paycheck is earmarked by the government for Social Security and Medicare at a rate of 7.65 percent. Of that percentage, 6.2 percent (of up to $68,400 of earned income) goes to Social Security, and the remaining 1.45 percent (of unlimited earnings) goes to Medicare. By law, the amount is matched by your employer.

If you are self-employed, you pay your own Social Security taxes when you pay your income taxes. The IRS then reports your earnings to Social Security. You have to pay both your own rate and the employer share so in essence you pay twice as much. However, there is a tax deduction you can take on the employer share.

Social Security is calculated on a "credit" basis. There are variations on this theme for part-time employees or people who do not work the full year. The general rule, however, is that for every $700 in income earned per quarter, you earn a credit. This amount rises gradually as the average income levels increase, but it is still a low amount. Anyone born after 1929 needs 40 credits to qualify for retirement benefits. If you were born prior to 1929, you need 1 credit less per year.

Those born after 1959 will need to be age 67 to obtain full benefits. Early retirement at age 62 is available for workers with sufficient credits, but benefits will be reduced by 20 to 30 percent for life.

A spouse of a retiree may also be eligible to receive family benefits if he or she is over 62 years of age. Widows or widowers may be eligible to receive survivor's benefits if they are at least 60 years old. Unmarried widows or widowers raising a child entitled to child's benefits may receive mother's or father's benefits. People of any age, who have had a steady income of at least $500 per month or a certain number of credits accrued depending on age, can receive Social Security disability payments if they become unable to work for an extended period of time.

For information, contact the Social Security Administration. Request form SSA-7004 to receive a copy of your Personal Earnings and Benefit Estimate Statement. Request this information every three or four years to double check that the records are current and accurate. It's your money, so you have a right to know that it is being handled correctly. If your employer is not taking out money for Social Security, let them know that as well. Don't wait until you are about to retire to check on your benefits. Their address is P.O. Box 17743, Baltimore, MD, 21235, 800/772-1213, or you can get information online at *www.ssa.gov.*

Medicare

Your Social Security office can provide you with Medicare information as well. Medicare provides basic health insurance to people age 65 or over who are entitled to Social Security benefits (even though they may not be receiving them), and to disabled people receiving Social Security disability payments for at least two years. People who require kidney dialysis or a kidney transplant may be eligible for Medicare at any age.

Medicare covers both medical and hospital insurance. The medical insurance (Part B) primarily covers doctor's fees, physical therapy, X-rays, and diagnostic tests. The hospital insurance portion (Part A) is for stays in the hospital or in a skilled nursing facility following a hospital stay. You can have the Medicare portion of your Social Security sent directly to a health maintenance organization (HMO), if you choose to use them as your service provider.

You can have Medicare questions answered by calling 800/772-1213. Medicare information may also be obtained online at *www.medicare.gov* and *www.hcfa.gov.*

Your Retirement Plan

The majority of Americans, even those with a pension plan, must take responsibility for the bulk of their retirement. How much money you need depends on your lifestyle, age of retirement, future plans, and other investments. It is estimated that you will need about 75 percent of your average income in your peak earning years, traditionally your 40s and 50s. Naturally, this also depends on what you do for a living. The bottom line in determining your retirement expenses is to look at your current budget and see how much you need to cover your expenses at present. Evaluate what expenses you will have at the age at which you plan to retire. Don't forget to increase the amount slightly in conjunction with the inflation rate.

Start to save for retirement sooner rather than later. The primary options when it comes to setting up retirement accounts include 401(k), IRA, SEP-IRA, and Keogh accounts. There are also defined benefit plans, profit sharing, and other lesser known plans.

401(k) Plans

Since their inception in 1981, 401(k) plans have made saving for retirement particularly easy; your employer sets up the account for you, and (if you choose to participate) your money is automatically transferred into it. Also, since you never see the money (contributions are usually made through salary deduction), you don't miss it, and you don't pay income taxes on it.

You are able to contribute up to a maximum of $10,000 of your salary into your 401(k). The plan providers can set up other specifications in conjunction with the company. In over 80 percent of companies with such plans, employers match a portion of the amount you put in by 25, 40, 50, or even (although rarely) 100 percent. Some plans are vested, meaning that you need to stay for x amount of years before you can benefit from the company-matched portion of the plan.

The 401(k) also gives you flexibility. You can choose how you want your money invested. Plans generally offer a few options including money market accounts, general growth or equity stock funds, or even stock in your own company. Different plans offer different options. Most of the time you can change these investments or the percentage of money allocated to each area.

Since 401(k) plans are for retirement, the one major restriction is that you leave the money in the account until you are 59 1/2 years of age or face a penalty upon withdrawal. However, in the case of some hardship situations, you can withdraw the money sooner without paying a penalty.

All in all, if a 401(k) plan is offered, you should take it. Reports show that in offices where such a plan is set up more than half of the employees utilize it, and the number should be higher. You do not pay tax on your 401(k) contributions, so if your company is matching your contribution at 50 percent, it's like getting at least a 50 percent return on your investment.

For nonprofit organizations such as schools and hospitals, a 403(b) plan is available to employees. Although this tax-sheltered plan is more limited in its investment options, it works on a similar basis to the 401(k) plan. Local and state governments offer a 457 plan. Rollovers on 457 plans may be restricted under state laws.

If you change jobs (by choice or not), you can roll over your 401(k) plan into the new company's plan; by law the employer has to allow you to do so. Or, you can roll the money into a rollover IRA account. It is to your advantage to have the money rolled over by a direct trustee-to-trustee transfer, thus avoiding any taxes. If you have the money sent directly to you, prior to putting it into another account, the company has to withhold 20 percent in a new account or the entire amount will be considered taxable income. If you can compensate for the 20 percent withheld for taxes when you open the new account, then none of the roll over will be taxable, thereby allowing the 20 percent that was withheld to be returned to you.

IRAs

For those who do not have 401(k) or 403(b) plans at their disposal, IRAs are the fashionable retirement plan. IRAs, or Individual Retirement Accounts, come in many configurations. The bottom line is that you can contribute up to $2,000 a year; a nonworking spouse may contribute an additional $2,000. Banks, mutual fund companies, and brokerage houses are among the places from which you can obtain an IRA.

A popular new type of IRA today is the Roth IRA. The Roth is not unlike the traditional IRA in terms of getting a plan started. However, you cannot take a tax deduction on a Roth as you can with the traditional IRA. On the other hand, there are advantages on the withdrawal end that are significant.

The Roth stipulates that the money remain in the plan until you are 59½; however, after five years, you can withdraw money without a penalty if you are disabled, if you use the distribution to pay up to $10,000 of qualifying first-time home buying expenses, or if the distribution is to the beneficiary following the death of the account owner.

The primary difference between a traditional IRA and a Roth IRA boils down to a question of now or later. Would you prefer to take a tax deduction now and to pay taxes later upon withdrawal, or would you prefer no deduction now but no taxes later? Evaluate this by your current income level and tax bracket. Also consider what your income will be upon retirement. All in all, a traditional or a Roth IRA is a strong retirement vehicle.

Two other IRAs are the SEP-IRA for self-employed persons and the Simple IRA for small businesses with income under $60,000. The SEP allows you to contribute 15 percent of your earned income up to $30,000; the Simple allows you to contribute up to the first $6,000 of earned income. These accounts are both light in paperwork.

Withdrawing Money from a Traditional IRA

You cannot withdraw money from an IRA without penalty until you reach the age of 59½. Like everything else in life, there are exceptions. These exceptions include money used for qualifying higher education, first-time home buying expenses, or substantial medical costs. Also, if you inherit the IRA from your spouse and maintain the distribution schedule of the deceased spouse or if you have certain disabilities that can be expected to last indefinitely, you can withdraw money without a penalty.

Once you hit 59½, it's up to you to withdraw your money as you see fit. However, once you hit 70½ it is mandatory that you start withdrawing your money, or you will face a stiff penalty.

Should you be holding an IRA (not a Roth IRA), the required annual withdrawal will be based on life expectancy depending on your age as determined by a government table. You need the total of the fair market value of all plan assets on the last day of the year and the appropriate divisor (based on age) from the government life expectancy table to calculate the amount of withdrawal for the current calendar year. If you do not meet the annual withdrawal minimum amount, you will pay a penalty of 50 percent of the amount you failed to withdraw.

If you are married, you can use a joint life expectancy table, which has a longer life expectancy than if you calculate for one person. If you use this double life expectancy, you have a higher divisor and lesser amount that you have to take out than if you use the single table.

If a person passes away, the spouse can roll over the IRA as the beneficiary. He or she may then continue taking the money out utilizing his or her own life expectancy or the joint life expectancy table if a "time certain" method of calculation was elected prior to the first withdrawal. A "time certain" method defines the number of years you are going to be making withdrawals in accordance with the government table.

Keogh Plans

In a Keogh plan, employers set aside money for themselves and their employees. After three years of work, at 1,000 hours or more per year, employees must be deemed eligible for coverage. Keogh plans, however, are most popular with those who are self-employed. You are allowed a maximum contribution as a self-employed individual of $30,000 per year. There are three types of Keogh plans, and additional constraints may be imposed depending on the type of plan.

In a profit sharing Keogh, annual contributions are limited to 15 percent but can be as low as 0 percent in a given year. In a money purchase Keogh, contributions are limited to 1 to 25 percent of compensation (but once set, they must continue for the life of the plan). A paired Keogh combines the terms of the profit sharing and money purchase plans. Keogh plans must be established by December 31st of the year for which you want to start making contributions, although you have until you file your tax return (which can be October 15th if on an extension) to make the contribution.

Like IRA and 401(k) plans, Keoghs have penalties for early withdrawal, or money taken out of the account before the age of 59½. Once you retire, you can have the money paid to you in monthly amounts or in one lump sum (both of which are taxable). Also, like the other plans, distributions must start by age 70½.

Since self-employment or any employment situation may change, you can rollover the money into an IRA. The roll over rules are similar to those of the 401(k) plan; a direct trustee-to-trustee transfer is recommended to avoid having to pay taxes.

The SEP (which was discussed earlier) is a variation on the Keogh; it can be easier to administer than the typical pension plan and beneficial to small businesses. Employers and employees both put money into this plan.

Defined Benefit Plan

A defined benefit plan is usually used by a small business when the principal is older, within ten years of retirement. You fund the benefit plan by figuring out what benefit would be payable on retirement, as if you were buying an annuity for someone at age 65. You are essentially planning backward, looking at what income you'll need later, and trying to figure out how you'll get there.

If you want to accumulate $200,000 in a finite number of years, you work backward and figure out how much you can put away each year and what additional return or interest you'll receive on your savings.

The annual contribution is not limited like it is in a profit sharing or a defined contribution plan. Benefits, however, are limited to $130,000, which is the government-imposed annual limit. You need to have your own documents and file with the IRS and the Department of Labor. Some banks sponsor defined benefit plans, as do brokerage houses. You would probably, however, go to a pension attorney or an actuary to set up such a plan.

Handling Money During Retirement

If you've done some proper planning in advance, you should be able to enjoy your retirement years while being assured that you have money available. While it is likely that your living expenses will be lower, you will still need to have a steady income. You've worked long and hard to get to this point; you should not have financial headaches during retirement.

You need to set up a budget in advance, as you did prior to retirement—the difference being that during retirement your income will be derived from money withdrawn from those retirement plans that you set up, plus Social Security and any pension you are entitled to. You might also think about part-time work to remain busy as well as to make some money. If you are able to equal 75 percent of your income prior to retirement, you should do well.

During the five to ten years approaching retirement, you should set up your retirement plan. Think about these questions:

1. What do you want to be doing during retirement?
2. Where do you want to be living?
3. What finances will be available?

Five Retirement Options to Consider

Many of the financial magazines, the planners, and the experts offer a host of new and inventive ways to invest your money. If you've worked many years to save up for retirement or you are trying to get by on a more limited amount of income/savings, this is not the time to get caught up in anything risky. However, with inflation, an approach that is too safe and conservative may have you falling behind.

Here are some suggestions you should consider, depending on how much money you are dealing with, your age, and your lifestyle. Remember, your goal is to be comfortable with the money you have coming in.

1. Keep at least the first $30,000 in a safe place, such as a bank CD, Treasury note, money market account, or other cash instrument.
2. Invest a high percentage of your portfolio in bond funds (through a broker or planner). If you want a steady stream of income, investing in high-yield bond funds is one way to achieve it. These funds can provide

a cushion you won't find with more high-risk equity funds.

3. Sell off the house, buy a condominiun, and put your money toward travel, grandchildren, and other things you desire.

4. Convert cash value life insurance into an annuity plan that pays monthly income. The money that built up during your working years when your family needed to be supported can now be better invested.

5. Keep an active portfolio. Again, this depends on your income and amount saved. However, if you have had a retirement plan—401(k) or pension—or accumulated any significant savings, you can maintain a diversified portfolio, only hedge toward the more conservative side.

Estate Planning

It's important that you plan your estate to suit your own personal wishes. After all, they're your assets. If you neglect estate planning entirely, you will be leaving the process up to the courts, who will not necessarily distribute the assets as you would have wished.

It's to your advantage to talk to an estate planning attorney or a professional financial planner. Planning strategy, often using credit shelter trusts and other methods of moving money around (such as gifting), can save a family hundreds of thousands of dollars in estate taxes. Comprehensive planners look at the overall situation of each person individually. Although planners and lawyers will cost you money, they can plan your estate in a manner that affords your heirs far greater protection.

The Will

The legal document that determines how your assets will be divided after your death is your will. The document should cover all assets including bank accounts, stocks, bonds, mutual funds, investments, real estate you own (including your home), and any and all other tangible property you own such as your car, boat, furniture, jewelry, art, and so on.

There are several types of wills that can be drawn up. A simple will has assets distributed outright to the beneficiaries. A young couple who draws up a will and bequeaths everything to each other have what is often termed a "sweetheart" will. A more complicated will may have testamentary trusts established to receive assets from the estate, or may transfer assets to a "pour over" trust created by another document.

It also should be mentioned that some people today are filing what is called a living will. Such wills provide medical and health care instructions to be carried out should you, for example, become physically incapacitated and require a life support system to stay alive. A health care power of attorney should be named in conjunction with a living will.

Probate

Probate is essentially the administering of the will by the court. The probate process first establishes whether there is a will. If a will exists, probate issues letters in conjunction with the document, appointing the executor. The executor then follows the wishes outlined by the deceased in his or her will. This is not always easy, as taxes may need to be paid and the money may not be there to pay them. In such a case, the executor may have to sell off some of the assets to raise the money to cover the taxes. There may also be challenges to the will by relatives of the deceased. Furthermore, property has to be valued correctly, which may require obtaining appraisals. Probate can take a long time, and whatever the executor does must be reviewed by the court.

Probate is something that many people seek to avoid for several reasons, some of which include:

- It is public record, and individuals with considerable wealth often want to keep the administration of their estate private. They also do not want people coming after their heirs looking for money.
- Probate is often a long, slow, tedious process that can drag on for years.
- Probate fees to an attorney and sometimes to the executor can mount over time.
- If you own homes or property in different states, there will be ancillary probate, which means probate will take place in those states as well.

Trusts

One of the most commonly used methods of avoiding probate is to put assets into a living trust. Trusts are the people who will receive the assets upon your death.

By placing your assets, including your house, into the trust, you maintain control while you are still living (as the trustee and beneficiary) and keep the assets outside of probate when you die. You will have to pay taxes on any income earned by the trust during your lifetime, and the assets held by a living trust are included in your estate for federal tax purposes.

Often a husband and wife open a jointly held revocable trust so that when one spouse dies, his or her half of the estate becomes irrevocable and goes to the remaining spouse. The part held by the remaining spouse is then revocable and can be altered. There is also a successor trustee named, should the spouse die or become incapacitated.

Irrevocable life insurance trusts purchase life insurance policies on individuals. The premiums are paid directly by the trust or by the future beneficiaries on behalf of the trust. The million dollars in a life insurance policy held by an insurance trust bypasses probate and is not taxed in the individual's estate. You can stipulate how and when the money will be dispensed to the beneficiaries, when forming the trust. The key factor is that it must be irrevocable.

Support trusts are designed to support your children and your spouse. They can be set up in any number of ways, detailing exactly how the income and trust principal should be distributed. The trustee can be given flexibility, or not, depending on the situation. This is also called a discretionary trust. The trust may give basic parameters and allow the trustee to use his or her judgment. For example, a person could set up a five-by-five plan allowing for $5,000 per month for needs and $5,000 per month for wants. A variation of the discretionary trust might tell the trustee to keep a tighter reign over the spending of the beneficiaries.

A credit shelter trust (also called a bypass trust) is a trust for those estates that go over the $625,000 exemption. Credit shelter trusts allow you to leave the highest amount of money that can go free of taxes to the trust when you die so that it doesn't go to the spouse and thus avoids taxation in the spouse's estate.

A qualified terminal interest property trust, also known as a Q-tip trust, is used often by people who have children from previous marriages and want to be sure that they are taken care of along with their second spouse and subsequent family.

A dynasty trust can continue for generations. It is often established as a generation-skipping trust, which uses the exemption from the tax on transfers that skip over a generation. It takes a skilled estate planner, perhaps working with a CPA, to put this together to avoid tax ramifications.

Gifting

Federal estate taxes kick in when your estate is valued at $625,000 or more (by the year 2007 this will rise to $1 million). A way to get money out of the estate to bring the total under the $625,000 magic number is to set up a system of "gifting" in which you give to each of those you choose $10,000 or less annually—the amount that can be given tax free. If you are married, you can elect to gift-split with your spouse, and raise that tax-free limit to $20,000, with half of the gift being attributed to each spouse.

However, if you give more than that amount to one person in one year during your lifetime, any amount over that $10,000 would come off of your $625,000 exemption. So if you gave someone a $50,000 gift in one year, the first $10,000 would be exempt from taxes, but your estate would be taxed at $585,000 ($625,000-$40,000).

You can also establish irrevocable trusts to which you make annual gifts in the name of your children or grandchildren. The appreciation of the trust assets will no longer be part of your estate. Another gift-giving strategy is for a grandparent to make tax-free educational gifts to his or her grandchild by paying the tuition directly to the private school or college. Gifting can be an effective way to distribute your assets and avoid high federal estate taxes.

chapter nine

Taxes

Income tax has been an inevitable part of living and working in America for generations. Tax returns are due April 15th. And, figuring out how much you owe and how you can owe less can be frustrating and time-consuming.

Along with federal income tax, in most states, you pay state income tax. Currently there are seven states that do not have a state income tax: Alaska, Florida, Nevada, South Dakota, Texas, Washington, and Wyoming. Florida, however, has an intangibles tax on the value of your investments.

The forms, supplied by the IRS, include the 1040, which is the most commonly used tax form. Tax forms can be obtained from the IRS, your local library or post office, some banks, or by calling 800/Tax-Form. You can now download most tax forms through the Internet at *www.irs.ustreas.gov*. You can also get forms by fax. Or check the tax booklet for the number of the form you need and call 703/368-9694.

Tax preparation should not begin in January, unless you have a relatively simple, straightforward financial picture. The more income you have, beyond that from an employer, the more organized you should be throughout the year. Keep paid bills, receipts, brokerage statements, home mortgage forms, and any other transactions filed and clearly marked throughout the year. Make sure to keep your W-2 form(s) on hand as well as any 1099s that are sent to you. If you are self-employed, you should receive a Form 1099 from each payer for any money you earned over $600.

Filling Out the Forms

Following the instructions is not always easy, which is why each year more and more Americans turn to tax preparers for assistance. If you do choose to tackle the return yourself, it's suggested that you use last year's return as your guide.

Proceed slowly and, if necessary, recheck your backup information (sales receipts, statements from banks or brokers, trade slips, etc.) to be sure your entries on the tax forms are correct. You need to compute your total income, then your adjusted gross income, or AGI, which is the number you will use most often while calculating itemized deductions. The AGI is calculated by deducting from your income certain expenses, also known as above-the-line expenses, including deductible IRA contributions, the medical savings account deduction, moving expenses, half of the self-employment tax, the self-employed health insurance deduction, contributions to Keogh and self-employed SEP and Simple plans, penalty paid on early withdrawal from savings accounts, and alimony paid.

Once you have calculated the AGI, you can then either take the standard deduction or your itemized deductions from schedule

A in your tax booklet. Determine which method is in your favor. If your itemized deductions amount to more than the standard deductions, by all means use the itemized total. These are among the schedule A itemized deductions:

- Medical deductions (beyond the first 7.5 percent of your AGI)
- State and local income taxes and real estate taxes paid
- Home mortgage and investment interest paid
- Gifts to charity (receipts are required for contributions of $250 or more)
- Casualty or loss from theft
- Unreimbursed business expenses and investment expenses (over 2 percent of your AGI)

Carefully review any deductions, making sure they fit the parameters. Also make sure you keep backup material in case this information is questioned. Use the previous year's deductions as a guide. Glaring changes, such as $2,000 in unreimbursed business expenses one year and $22,000 the next, will attract attention, so be especially careful to have documented evidence of any major changes in your deductions.

Once you've completed your deductions, subtract your personal exemptions and compute your taxable income. The tax calculation formula would look like this:

1. Gross income minus adjustments or above-the-line deductions equals adjusted gross income (AGI).
2. AGI minus itemized or standard deductions minus personal exemptions equals taxable income

After the tax is computed, additional credits can reduce the tax. They are listed on Form 1040 and include a credit for child and dependent care expenses, a credit for the elderly or the disabled, an adoption credit (for expenses), and a foreign tax credit. Also, there is a credit for each child under age 17.

Reducing and Avoiding Taxes

There are three primary ways to reduce taxes:

1. Minimize what would be your gross annual income by finding tax-free investments in which to put your money.
2. Take as many itemized deductions as allowable.
3. Earn less money and fall into a lower tax bracket.

Tax-Free Investments

There are a number of legal ways (some of which are mentioned in various sections of the book) to defer taxes or to avoid taxes altogether. Both 401(k) and 403(b) retirement plans, as well as some IRAs, allow you to put away some of your income before paying taxes on it. Depending on the plan, however, you may have to pay taxes when you withdraw the money. This isn't necessarily a bad thing, since your income level during retirement may be less than it is now. U.S. Treasury bills and U.S. Treasury bonds are places to invest money to avoid state taxes, and municipal bonds are tax exempt for federal purposes, and for state purposes in the states in which they are issued.

Compensation that is paid in the form of benefits by your employer for hospitalization, group life insurance, other health plans, or dependent care is not taxable, subject to certain limitations. Furthermore, if you are reimbursed for money spent in direct relation to your employment (e.g., if you are reimbursed for dinner expenses incurred because you had to work late), such payments are not taxable. Also, under flexible spending plans, you can reduce your taxable income by making tax-free salary contributions to plans for reimbursement of expenses for medical or dependent care.

Quarterly Versus Yearly Payments

Filing your tax return and paying taxes are two different things. Companies, self-employed individuals, and anyone who has money coming in (that would result in $1,000 or more in taxes) should pay quarterly estimated taxes. Otherwise they pay interest and penalties, which explains why some people find the taxes they owe (on April 15th) to be higher than they anticipated.

If your paycheck is your only source of income, then your employer is withholding taxes for you, in which case you can skip this section. However, if you receive dividends, interest, capital gains, and other income, you, too, should be paying estimated taxes, unless the total tax liability is within $1,000 of the taxes withheld by your employer.

Estimated taxes for the current year are based on the actual tax from the previous year, less the withholdings. If you paid $12,000 in taxes last year, you can pay quarterly taxes at that same amount for the present year, or $3,000 per quarter. This can be helpful if in the second quarter of the year you suddenly make an extra $100,000. For that quarter, you can still pay $3,000 in estimated taxes, as you are protected from penalties by equaling or exceeding one fourth of last year's tax.

When paying quarterly taxes, you can also compute an annualized taxable income each quarter and pay the tax based on that amount. For example, if you have $10,000 of taxable net income in the first quarter of the year, you could pay that quarterly payment based on making $40,000 for the whole year. If you have an income that is seasonal and is higher in the latter part of the year, you might choose to do this. You can do this for each quarterly payment.

For example, if in the first quarter you earn $10,000 and in the second quarter you earn $5,000, you can then annualize for your second payment based on $15,000. Keep in mind, however, that the quarterly breakdown of tax payments is not even; the breakdown, as listed previously, falls after 3, 5, 8, and 12 months. Therefore, you would calculate your second "quarterly" payment based on 5 months. So, $15,000, annualized for your June 15th (second quarter) payment, would be taxed based on an annualized income of $36,000. An easy way to calculate this is to see how much one month would be and then multiply by the number of months you are up to at the end of that quarter (3, 5, 8, or 12). For example, $15,000 in five months is $3,000 per month or annualized at $36,000, from which you would base your second estimated tax payment. Compute your total annual tax on $36,000. Calculate 5/12 of that amount, which is your total cumulative liability to that point. Then subtract the amount you paid in your prior payment, and you will arrive at your current amount due.

Extensions

Anyone can get a six-month extension to file their form. Contrary to popular belief, this does not mean you don't have to pay the approximate balance of tax due by the April 15th filing date, plus quarterly tax estimates due for the current year. It just means that you can delay filing the return.

Too many people think an extension, like postponing jury duty, means you can forget about the situation entirely. This is not true, since you're still expected to pay. Therefore, don't utilize an extension unless it is absolutely necessary (e.g., to gather or locate more information, illness, or being out of the country).

State and Local Taxes

The general rule of thumb is to do your federal return first and then use most of the same information for your state return. But, before the tax year ends, estimate your full state tax liability and arrange for payment by December 31st if you can use "state taxes paid" as an itemized deduction.

Each state has a Department of Revenue, usually located in the state capital, that can answer your questions regarding state taxes and provide you with any paperwork you may need. If you are a resident of more than one state, are working in one state while living in another, move from one state to another, or work or receive income from more than one state, you may have to figure out several sets of state tax laws. One of the best places to seek out individual state-by-state information is at *www.taxweb.com*. This Web site can provide you with easy access to information.

Working with the IRS

The Internal Revenue Service, no matter what you think of it, does provide explanations (call 800/TAX-FORM or go online at *www.irs.ustreas.gov*), several free publications, and other information about the tax returns you will be filling out. If your return is not very complicated you can use the guidelines and file your own return.

Should you be called in for an audit, you need to organize your paperwork. You should also call your accountant, if you have one. The IRS will inform you of when they want to see you and specify what part of your return (and what year or years) they want to audit.

Make sure you can clearly explain your deductions and exactly what each receipt is for. Give yourself some time to prepare, in case you need to track down certain documents. Make sure you have copies of everything.

Additional Information

The previous chapters have provided a brief summary of several aspects of personal finance to help you manage, maintain, and invest your money. However, as you begin to create your own money management system, you may find that you require further guidance pertaining to a particular area. The following are recommended sources for additional information should you need it.

Financial Web Sites

Besides the sites offered by financial institutions and mutual fund families are Web sites set up by the leading financial magazines. Most of the magazine sites offer information on investing, home buying, and other significant areas of personal finance. Naturally, many sites give advice and suggestions on the latest stocks and funds to buy. Read advice tips carefully and look for second opinions before jumping to buy or sell. Some sites require you to pay to be hooked up with the latest daily stock quotes. This service is usually for the more advanced investors.

Here are just a few of the leading financial Web sites:

- Equity Analytics, Ltd. at *www.e-analytics.com*
- Invest-o-rama at *www.investorama.com*
- Microsoft Investor at *www.investor.com*
- Morningstar at *www.morningstar.com*
- Motley Fool at *www.fool.com*
- Personal Finance Magazine at *www.moneynet.com*
- Zacks investment research at *www.ultra.zacks.com*

Retirement Planning Information

While there are numerous Web sites and software programs dedicated to finance, savings, and investing, these four are devoted more specifically to retirement planning:

- American Express (*www.americanexpress.com/401K*) focuses on 401(k) plans and how they work. They provide easy-to-follow information about calculating the amount you need to invest to reach your desired amounts.
- T. Rowe Price (*www.troweprice.com/retirement*) offers concise, easy-to-follow listings and explanations of the many retirement plan options from IRAs to more complex plans for small business owners.

- Vanguard Retirement Planner is one of the leading software programs that can help you chart and plan for your retirement. It is widely available.
- Quicken Financial Planner is another leading software program that can help you plan for retirement. It, too, is widely available.

American Association of Individual Investors

The American Association of Individual Investors (AAII) is an independent nonprofit organization. For more than 20 years, it has been helping individuals to invest their own money.

Through various publications, videos, and seminars, the various chapters of AAII help over 175,000 current members by focusing on investing and investment techniques. Their guidance helps both new and seasoned investors and is not limited to those with large sums of money. They are, essentially, a professional association for non-professionals.

The $49 membership entitles you to their journal, which is published 10 times annually and offers how-to articles and information on investing. Perhaps the best feature of the journal is its objectivity; it is not sponsored by investment companies and does not recommend specific investments.

Also included in the membership is an annual guide to mutual funds, annual reports, educational material, and other publications. There are 70 local chapters and several ways to contact AAII: 312/280-0170 (membership services); 800/428-2244 (seminar registration and product information); *www.aaii.com* or aaii@aol.com (Keyword AAII).

There are also several books available from AAII including *The Individuals Investor's Guide to Low Load Mutual Funds*, *Investing Basics and Beyond*, *Stock Investing Basics*, *Portfolio Building Basics*, and others.

National Association of Personal Finance Advisors

The National Association of Personal Finance Advisors (NAPFA) is a membership association dedicated to helping the public receive impartial fee-based financial advice from qualified experts in the field. Members must submit a financial plan, meet educational requirements (including strict continuing education requirements), and work on a fee-only basis. NAPFA members should provide comprehensive information on a broad cross section of issues. The only organization of its kind, NAPFA has nearly 600 members throughout the United States. You can contact NAPFA to meet with a financial planner by calling 888/366-2732.

Tax Information

Some places to seek help, besides tax books in the library, include a couple of leading tax software programs: Turbo Tax Deluxe from Intuit (MacInTax for Mac users; or use their online tax preparation service at *www.webturbotax.com*) and TaxCut Deluxe from *Kiplingers*.

Besides the IRS Web site, you can go online and get information from *www.hrblock.com/tax*. The H&R Block site includes new tax laws, ways to itemize, and a calculator for determining your refund.

One of the more interesting books, although not easy reading, is Jeff Schnepper's annual *How to Pay Zero Taxes*. Probably the most thorough book you can buy is J. K. Lasser's *Your Income Tax Guide*, which comes out annually. J. K. Lasser also offers a monthly tax newsletter. You can contact them at 815-734-1104.

index

401(k) plans, 86–87, 102
403(b) plans, 87, 102

a

AGI (adjusted gross income), 100, 101
America Online, 44
American Association of Individual
　Investors (AAII), 109–10
American Express, 16–17, 108
Ameritrade, 60
Annuity plans, 93
ATM cards, 18–19, 38, 42
Audits, 105

b

Balanced funds, 70–71
Banking, 35–45
　account types, 35–40
　choosing a bank, 41–42
　computer programs for, 10–11, 44
　online, 44–45
Bankruptcy, 31–33
Blue chip stock, 49
Bonds, 69–70, 77–82
　price of, 78
　ratings, 82
　types of, 79–82
Boston Equiserve, 56
Brokerage houses, 54, 56–59
Budgets, 1–11
　calculating, 6–8
　categories for, 2–6
　computer programs for, 10–11
　sample of, 7
　for shopping, 8–10
Bureau of Public Debt, 41, 79
Bypass trusts, 96

c

Capital gains, 103
Cash accounts, 36
CDs (certificates of deposit), 36, 39–40,
　70, 92
Charles Schwab, 60
Chase Mellon, 56
Checking accounts, 38–39, 43–44
CitiBank, 45
CNN, 52
Common stocks, 50
Computer programs, 10–11, 44, 108, 110
Corporate bonds, 81
Credit bureaus, 20–22
Credit cards, 13–23
　advantages of, 13
　assistance with, 30–31
　choosing, 15–19
　delinquencies, 22–23
　disadvantages of, 13–14
　fees, 15–16
　lost cards, 19
　paying off, 28
　stolen cards, 19
　terms and conditions, 15–16
　types of, 17–19
Credit fixers, 30
Credit rating, 19–23
Credit reports, 20, 21, 33
Credit shelter trusts, 93, 96
Cyclical stocks, 49

d

Debit cards, 18–19
Debt, 25–33
　alternatives, 29–30
　assistance with, 30–31
　avoiding, 26–27

bankruptcy, 31–33
  eliminating, 27–29
Debt versus credit limit, 22–23
Deductions, 100–102, 105
Defined benefit plan, 91
Department of Labor, 91
Department of Revenue, 105
DIPs (Dividend Investment Plans), 55–56
Discover Card, 17
Discretionary trusts, 96
Disney, 49
Diversification, 65–66, 93
Dividend Investment Plans (DIPs), 55–56
Dividend Reinvestment Plans (DRPs), 55–56
Dividends, 55–56, 103
Dow Jones Industrial Average, 53, 62
DRPs (Dividend Reinvestment Plans), 55–56
Dynasty trust, 97

e

EE savings bonds, 80
Equifax, 20, 21
Equities, 48, 51
Equity Analytics, Ltd., 108
Estate planning, 93–97
Estimated taxes, 103–4
E*Trade, 60
Excel, 10
Executors, 94–95
Experian, 20, 21

f

Fannie Mae, 79, 80
FDIC (Federal Deposit Insurance Corporation), 35, 36, 40, 42
Federal income tax, 99–100, 103–4
Federal Trade Commission, 22
Financial guidance, 107–11
Financial Web sites, 107–10
Fixed income mutual funds, 66–67
FNN, 52, 56
Forbes, 65
Freddie Mac, 80

g

General Motors, 49
Gifting, 93, 97

Ginnie Mae, 79, 80
GNMA (Government National Mortgage Association), 79, 80
Government bonds, 79–80
Growth stocks, 49–50, 67, 68

h

H&R Block, 110
Health insurance, 85, 102
HH savings bonds, 80
High-yield bonds, 81–82
HMO (health maintenance organization), 85
How to Pay Zero Taxes, 111

i

IBC, 72
IBM, 49
Income stocks, 49–50, 68–69
Income tax, 99–100, 103–4
Individuals Investor's Guide to Low Load Mutual Funds, 110
Insurance, 85, 96, 102
Intangibles tax, 99
Interest rates, 15–16, 37, 78
International stock funds, 69
Intuit Quicken, 10, 44
Invest-o-rama, 108
Investing Basics and Beyond, 110
Investments, 36, 47–63. *See also* Mutual Funds; Stocks
  assistance with, 109–10
  retirement and, 92–93
  risks, 47, 50, 57, 62, 66–68
IPO (initial public offering), 48–49
IRAs (Individual Retirement Accounts), 87, 88–89, 102
Irrevocable trusts, 96–97
IRS (Internal Revenue Service), 83, 91, 99, 105
Itemized deductions, 100–102, 105

j

Junk bonds, 81–82

k

Keogh plans, 90
Kiplingers, 65, 71

l

Lasser, J. K., 111
Life insurance, 96
Living wills, 94
Load funds, 71–72
Lotus, 10

m

MacInTax, 110
Managing Your Money, 10, 44
Margin accounts, 54
MasterCard, 16–17
MECA Software, 10
Medicare, 83, 85
Microsoft Investor, 108
Microsoft Money, 10, 44
Money, 65, 73
Money Fund Report, 72
Money market deposit accounts (MMDAs), 39, 92
Money market mutual funds, 66–67, 69, 70, 72
Moody's, 82
Morningstar, 108
Mortgage-backed bonds, 80
Motley Fool, 108
Municipal bonds, 80–81
Mutual funds, 48, 65–75. *See also* Stocks
    choosing, 66, 73
    risks of, 66–68
    tracking, 74–75
    types of, 68–72

n

NASDAQ Composite Index, 53
National Association of Personal Finance Advisors (NAPFA), 110
National Association of Securities Dealers (NASD), 58–59
National Foundation for Consumer Credit (NFCC), 30
NAV (net asset value), 74
No-load funds, 71–72
NOW accounts, 36, 38

o

Online banking, 44–45. *See also* Banking
Online trading, 54, 59–61. *See also* Stocks

p

Passbook accounts, 37
Pension plan, 85
Personal Finance Magazine, 108
Portfolio Building Basics, 110
Pour-over trusts, 94
Preferred stocks, 50
Probate, 94–95. *See also* Estate planning
Procter & Gamble, 49
Prospectus, 72–73

q

Q-tip trust, 96
Qualified terminal interest property trust, 96
Quarterly taxes, 103–4
Quicken, 10, 44
Quicken Financial Planner, 109

r

Retirement planning, 83–97
    assistance with, 108–9
    investments and, 92–93
    money management, 91–92
    taxes and, 87–90, 100, 102
    tips, 92–93
    types of plans, 86–91
Revocable trust, 95–96
Roth IRA, 88

s

S&P (Standard & Poor's), 53, 82
Sallie Mae (Student Loan Marketing Association), 80
Savings accounts, 36
Savings bonds, 80
Schnepper, Jeff, 111
Secured credit cards, 18
Securities, 66
Securities Act of 1933, 48
Securities and Exchange Commission (SEC), 48–49, 52, 59, 72
Securities Investor Protection Corporation (SIPC), 58
SEP-IRA, 88
Shareholders, 51, 66
Social Security, 83–85. *See also* Retirement planning
Standard & Poor's (S&P), 53, 82
State income tax, 99, 105

Statement accounts, 37
Stock brokers, 54, 56–59. *See also* Stocks
Stock Investing Basics, 110
Stock market indicators, 53
Stock market volatility, 47, 67, 75
Stocks, 47–63. *See also* Mutual funds
    brokerage fees, 54, 56, 58
    buying, 51–57
    choosing, 52–53
    online trading, 54, 59–61
    selling, 52
    strategies, 61–63
    tips, 56–57
    types of, 68–69
Student Loan Marketing Association
    (Sallie Mae), 80
Support trusts, 96

t

T. Rowe Price, 108
TaxCut Deluxe, 110
Taxes, 99–105
    assistance with, 110–11
    avoiding, 102–3
    computer programs for, 110
    deductions, 100–102, 105
    estate planning and, 93, 97
    extensions, 104
    forms, 99–102
    organizing, 100
    quarterly, 103–4
    reducing, 102–3
    retirement planning and, 87–90,
        100, 102
    returns, 99, 103–4
    state, 99, 105
Tax-free investments, 69–70, 80–81, 102–3
T-bills (Treasury bills), 40–41, 102
TD Waterhouse Group, 60
Testamentary trusts, 94
Trans Union LLC, 20, 22
Treasury bills (T-bills), 40–41, 102
Treasury bonds, 79–80, 102
Treasury Department, 41
Treasury notes, 92
Trustees, 95–96
Trusts, 39, 93–97. *See also* Estate planning
Turbo Tax Deluxe, 110

u

United States Postal Service, 80
USA Today, 52, 56

v

Vanguard Retirement Planner, 109
VISA card, 16–17

w

Wall Street Journal, 52, 56, 65, 71
Web sites, financial, 107–10
Wills, 94. *See also* Estate planning

y

Your Income Tax Guide, 111

z

Zacks Investment Research, 108
Zero coupon bonds, 79–80